E-Learning QUICK Checklist

Badrul Khan
George Washington University, USA

WITHDRAWN

TOURO COLLEGE LIBRARY
Main Campus Midtown

Information Science Publishing

Hershey • London • Melbourne • Singapore

MT

Acquisitions Editor:	Mehdi Khosrow-Pour
Senior Managing Editor:	Jan Travers
Managing Editor:	Amanda Appicello
Development Editor:	Michele Rossi
Copy Editor:	Maria Boyer

Published in the United States of America by
    Information Science Publishing (an imprint of Idea Group Inc.)
    701 E. Chocolate Avenue
    Hershey PA 17033
    Tel: 717-533-8845
    Fax: 717-533-8661
    E-mail: cust@idea-group.com
    Web site: http://www.idea-group.com

and in the United Kingdom by
    Information Science Publishing (an imprint of Idea Group Inc.)
    3 Henrietta Street
    Covent Garden
    London WC2E 8LU
    Tel: 44 20 7240 0856
    Fax: 44 20 7379 3313
    Web site: http://www.eurospan.co.uk

Copyright © 2005 by Idea Group Inc. All rights reserved. No part of this book may be reproduced in any form or by any means, electronic or mechanical, including photocopying, without written permission from the publisher.

ISBN 1-59140-812-1 paperback

eISBN 1-59140-811-3

E-Learning QUICK Checklist is an abbreviated version of the IGI book, *Managing E-Learning: Design, Delivery, Implementation and Evaluation*, by Badrul Khan. Copyright 2005; ISBN 1-59140-634-X (h/c), ISBN 1-59140-635-8 (s/c), ISBN 1-59140-636-6 (ebook). For more information on this book, visit the IGI website at www.idea-group.com.

British Cataloguing in Publication Data
A Cataloguing in Publication record for this book is available from the British Library.

All work contributed to this book is new, previously-unpublished material. The view expressed in this book are those of the author, but not necessarily of the publisher.

09/23/05

E-Learning Quick Checklist

Table of Contents

Preface

With the advent of the Internet and online learning methodologies and technologies, providers of education and training are creating learning materials to fulfill the demand. The Internet and digital technologies combined with appropriate learning strategies help to create open, dynamic and flexible learning environments with implications for countless applications with respect to education and training. Academic institutions, corporations, and government agencies worldwide are increasingly using the Internet and digital technologies to deliver instruction and training.

What does it take to create an open, flexible and distributed learning environment for diverse learners? Well, a learning environment should be meaningful to all stakeholder groups, including learners, instructors, support services staff, and the institution. It is meaningful to *learners* when it is easily accessible, well-designed, learner-centered, affordable, efficient and flexible, and has a facilitated learning environment. When learners display a high level of participation and success in meeting a course's goals and objectives, learning becomes meaningful for *instructors*. In turn, when learners enjoy all available support services provided in the course without any interruptions, it makes *support services staff* happy as they strive to provide easy-to-use, reliable services. Finally, a learning system is meaningful to *institutions* when it has a sound return on investment (ROI), a moderate to high level of learner satisfaction with both the quality of instruction and all support services, and a low drop-out rate.

To create a meaningful open, flexible and distributed learning environment for diverse learners, we must explore important issues encompassing various dimensions of e-learning environment. To understand the critical dimensions of e-learning environments, since 1997 I have been communicating with learners, instructors, trainers, administrators, and technical and other support services staff involved in e-learning, in both academic and corporate settings, all over the world. I have researched e-learning issues discussed in professional discussion forums, newspapers, magazines, and journals, and I have designed and taught online courses. Also, as the editor of *Web-Based Training* (Educational Technology Publications, 2001) and the forthcoming *Flexible Learning* (Educational Technology Publications), I have had the opportunity to work closely on critical e-learning issues with more than 100 authors worldwide who contributed chapters to these books.

Through these activities, I found that numerous factors help to create a meaningful learning environment, and many of these factors are systemically interrelated and interdependent. A systemic understanding of these factors can help us create meaningful flexible and distributed learning environments. I clustered these factors into eight categories: institutional, management, technological, pedagogical, ethical, interface design, resource support, and evaluation. I found these eight categories to be logically comprehensive and empirically the most useful dimensions for open, flexible and distributed learning environments.

The *purpose of the* **E-Learning Quick Checklist** book is to walk you through the various factors (encompassing these eight dimensions) important to developing, evaluating, and implementing open, flexible and distributed learning environments. This book is designed as a Quick Checklist for e-learning. It contains many practical items that you can use as review criteria to check if e-learning modules, courses and programs provide the level of services that learners (or consumers) should expect. Items in the checklist encompass the critical dimensions of an e-learning environment, including pedagogical, technological, interface design, evaluation, management, resource support, ethical, and institutional. Throughout this book, various critical e-learning and blended-learning factors are presented as questions or items that you can ask yourself when planning, designing, evaluating, and implementing e-learning and/ or blended-learning modules, courses, and programs.

This book has eight sections based on the eight dimensions. Numerous factors discussed in sections 1-8 should give you a comprehensive picture of open, flexible and distributed learning and should also help you think through every aspect of what you are doing during the various steps of e-learning process. Within the scope of this checklist book, only some critical items or questions related to each dimension of the e-learning environment are presented as examples; they (i.e., the items) are thus by no means complete. There are a myriad of important items or questions encompassing the various dimensions of an e-learning environment that need to be explored. Please note that each e-learning project is unique. I encourage you to identify as many issues as possible for your own e-learning project under each dimension.

You may be thinking—*how many issues do I have to address? how many issues are necessary?* It depends on the goals and scope of your project. The more e-learning issues you explore and address, the more meaningful and supportive a learning environment you help to create for your target population.

Designing open, flexible, and distributed learning systems for diverse learners is challenging; however, as more and more institutions offer e-learning to learners worldwide, we will become more knowledgeable about what works and what does not work. We should try our best to accommodate the needs of stakeholder groups by asking as many critical questions as possible along the eight dimensions of e-learning environment. The number and types of questions may vary based on each unique e-learning system. Given our specific e-learning contexts, we may not be able to address all the critical issues within the eight dimensions of e-learning. We should find ways to address them with the best possible means that we can afford. It is important to ask as many questions as possible during the planning period of e-learning design.

Who can benefit from this checklist? I believe a wide range of people can use the book. Here is the list of people who I think can benefit from the issues discussed in the book:

- *Instructors* can use this checklist in courses such as distance education, e-learning, blended learning, online education, Web-based instruction, distributed learning, computers in education, hypermedia, multimedia, educational technology, instructional technology, educational telecommunications, teacher training, corporate training, etc.

- *Instructors, teachers, trainers, training managers, distance education specialists, e-learning specialists, virtual education specialists, e-learning project managers, instructional designers, corporate education specialists, human resources specialists, performance technologists, educational technology coordinators, media specialists, webmasters, writers/editors and technical support staff* can use this checklist to plan, design, evaluate, and implement e-learning and blended learning modules, courses, and programs.

- *Virtual/corporate university designers* can use this checklist to plan, design, evaluate, and implement corporate/virtual universities.

- *School administrators, higher education administrators, department of education staff, ministry of education staff, virtual and corporate university administrators, human resources managers and consultants* can use this checklist to develop strategic plans for designing, evaluating and implementing e-learning initiatives.

- *Providers of e-learning* (schools, colleges, universities, training and other institutions) can use this quick checklist to understand the level of services that learners (or consumers) expect in e-learning.

- *Accrediting agencies* can use this quick checklist to review whether e-learning providers provide high-quality instruction and good support services that learners must have. *Department of education and ministry of education staff* can use this quick checklist to develop criteria for new grant initiatives for e-learning related projects.

- *Anyone contemplating a career in training and development, curriculum planning, and Internet applications* can use this book to learn about e-learning and blended learning design strategies.

Finally, I hope that items encompassing the various critical dimensions of e-learning and blended learning issues included in this checklist will help you understand all aspects of open, flexible, and distributed learning environment and provide valuable guidance in creating e-learning and blended learning experience for your target audience. I would appreciate hearing your comments regarding this book.

Badrul Huda Khan
bhk@BooksToRead.com
Website: http://BadrulKhan.com/khan

Acknowledgments

This book owes much to the encouragement and assistance of many people. First to the people at Idea Group Inc., who encouraged me to publish this checklist in support of the many organizations currently striving to implement or improve their e-learning programs. I would especially like to recognize the senior acquisitions editor, Mehdi Khosrow-Pour for his vision and foresight for the need for this book.

I would like to thank my graduate students at the George Washington University who used the first draft of this checklist for a graduate course on critical issues in distance education. Their feedback as students and "users" were invaluable. I would also like to thank many colleagues and reviewers for their comments and suggestions and in particular David Peal, for his critical review and helpful feedback. I would like to thank Larry Lipsitz, (editor of *Educational Technology* magazine) for his continued support. I am also indebted to Myunghee Kang for her valuable comments. I would also like to thank Ruth Bennett for her review.

I would also like to thank many of my well-wishers who believed in me and were always there when I needed them: Fakhrul Ahsan, Saleha Begum, Anisur R. Khan, Maung Sein, Qamrul Islam and Syeda Munim.

Finally, and most important, I thank my wife Komar Khan and my sons Intisar Khan and Inshat Khan; my brothers Kamrul H. Khan, Manzurul H. Khan and Nazrul H. Khan, and my sisters Nasima Zaman and Akhtar Janhan Khanam; my cousins Mahmudul Alam and Masud Ul Alam and my niece Sabrina Zaman Choudhury for their continued support and encouragements. I would also like to thank all my nieces and nephews for their encouragement.

This book is dedicated to my late parents:

Mr. Lokman Khan Sherwani &
Mrs. Shabnom Khanam Sherwani
of
Khan Manzil, Pathantooly, Chittagong, Bangladesh

INSTITUTIONAL

Needs Assessment

Does the institution conduct a survey to identify whether e-learning is suitable for learners?
- ❏ Yes
- ❏ No
- ❏ Not applicable
- ❏ Other (specify)

Does the institution conduct a need analysis for e-learning?
- ❏ Yes
- ❏ No
- ❏ Not applicable
- ❏ Other (specify)

If *yes*, check all that apply:
- ❏ To identify e-learning needs
- ❏ To identify technological needs for e-learning environment
- ❏ To identify other support services needs for e-learning environment
- ❏ To identify customers' (i.e., learners') willingness to take e-learning courses from the institution
- ❏ Not applicable
- ❏ Other (specify)

Financial Readiness

Is the e-learning initiative aligned with the institution's mission?
- ❏ Yes
- ❏ No
- ❏ Not applicable
- ❏ Other (specify)

Is the institution financially ready to venture into e-learning?
- ❏ Yes
- ❏ No
- ❏ Not applicable
- ❏ Other (specify)

Does the e-learning initiative have direct support from the senior administrative staff of the institution?
- ❏ Yes
- ❏ No
- ❏ Not applicable

❑ Other (specify)

Is the e-learning initiative dependent on financial sources?
❑ Yes
❑ No
❑ Not applicable
❑ Other (specify)
If *yes*, check all the apply:
    ❑ Internal funds from the institution
    ❑ Tuition and fees from students
    ❑ External funds from (check all that apply)
        ❑ Federal or national government
        ❑ State or provincial government
        ❑ County or district government
        ❑ Industry
        ❑ Foundation
        ❑ Other (specify)

Does the institution have adequate funds for e-learning?
❑ Yes
❑ No
❑ Not applicable
❑ Other (specify)

Does the institution have a timeline associated with how funds will be available during various phases of the e-learning initiative?
❑ Yes
❑ No
❑ Not applicable
❑ Other (specify)
If funds are not available as expected, does the institution have a plan that can eliminate not-so-critical areas of the e-learning initiative?
    ❑ Yes
    ❑ No
    ❑ Not applicable
    ❑ Other (specify)

Infrastructure Readiness

Does the institution have adequate human resources to support the e-learning initiative?
❑ Yes
❑ No

❏ Not applicable
❏ Other (specify)
If yes, check all that apply:
    ❏ Help desk staff
    ❏ Technical support staff
    ❏ Training staff to train e-learning staff
    ❏ Other (specify)

Does the institution have adequate equipment to support the e-learning initiative?
❏ Yes
❏ No
❏ Not applicable
❏ Other (specify)

Check appropriate hardware available for the role of each individual listed below.
Check all that apply (put "NA" if not applicable).

Role of Individual	Hardware																				
	Desktop Computer			Laptop Computer			PDA			Pager / Cellular Telephone			Printer / Scanner			Digital Camera / WebCam			Other (specify)		
	Work	Home	Mobile	Work	Home	Mobile	Work	Home	Mobile	Work	Home	Mobile	Work	Home	Mobile	Work	Home	Mobile	Work	Home	Mobile
Learner																					
Instructor (full-time)																					
Instructor (part-time)																					
Trainer																					
Trainer Assistant																					
Tutor																					
Technical Support																					
Help Desk																					
Librarian																					
Counselor																					
Graduate Assistant																					
Administrator																					
Other (specify)																					

Check appropriate Internet connection types available for the role of each individual listed below. Check all that apply (put "NA" if not applicable).

Role of Individual	Internet Connections																				
	Dial-Up			ISDN			Satellite Dish			Cable Modem			DSL			T1			Wireless / Other (specify)		
	Work	Home	Mobile	Work	Home	Mobile	Work	Home	Mobile	Work	Home	Mobile	Work	Home	Mobile	Work	Home	Mobile	Work	Home	Mobile
Learner																					
Instructor (full-time)																					
Instructor (part-time)																					
Trainer																					
Trainer Assistant																					
Tutor																					
Technical Support																					
Help Desk																					
Librarian																					
Counselor																					
Graduate Assistant																					
Administrator																					
Other (specify)																					

Check appropriate computer skills and familiarity with computer technology by the role of each individual listed below. Check all that apply (put "NA" if not applicable).

Role of Individual	Computer Skills and Computer Usage																					
	Word Processing			Internet Connectivity			Browsing			Familiarity with the Use of Audio and Video on the Internet			Familiarity with Computer Terms and Jargon			Years of Computer Usage				Other (specify)		
	Yes	No	NA	Yes	No	NA	Yes	No	NA	Yes	No	NA	None	1-2 Years	2-5 Years	Yes	No	NA	Yes	No	NA
Learner																					
Instructor (full-time)																					
Instructor (part-time)																					
Trainer																					
Trainer Assistant																					
Tutor																					
Technical Support																					
Help Desk																					
Librarian																					
Counselor																					
Graduate Assistant																					
Administrator																					
Other (specify)																					

Check the availability of appropriate hardware and software by the institution for e-learning. Check all that apply:

Hardware and Software	Availability			
	Yes	No	NA	Other (specify)
Servers				
Database				
Learning Management System (LMS)				
Learning Content Management System (LCMS)				
Enterprise Software				
Other (specify)				

How much experience does any of the following have with the on-line learning environment? Check all that apply:

Role of Individual	Experience Level			
	None	Some	Adequate	Other (specify)
Learner				
Instructor (full-time)				
Instructor (part-time)				
Teaching Assistant				
Tutor				
Technical Support				
Help Desk				
Librarian				
Counselor				
Graduate Assistant				
Administrator				
Other (specify)				

Does the institution use any of the following methods to identify the assistive technology and other support that disabled students may need to participate in e-learning? Check all that apply:

Methods	Yes	No	NA	Other (specify)
Interview				
Observation				
Document Review				
Survey				
Other (specify)				

Does the institution have a plan to train its staff for any new technological skills that they might need in the future?
- ❏ Yes
- ❏ No
- ❏ Not applicable
- ❏ Other (specify)

If *yes*, check all that apply:
- ❏ Full-time training staff
- ❏ Part-time training staff
- ❏ Planned full-time training staff
- ❏ Planned part-time training staff
- ❏ Staff are sent to get training from outside

❑ Outside consultants train its staff
❑ Other (specify)

If necessary technological skills are lacking, what steps will the institution take to speed up acquiring the skill?

_____

Cultural Readiness

Is any of the following ready for e-learning? (Note: It may be beneficial for the institution to name individual(s) or appoint a group responsible for identifying the cultural readiness of the following individuals.)

Role of Individual	Ready for E-Learning			
	Yes	No	NA	Other (specify)
Learner				
Instructor (full-time)				
Instructor (part-time)				
Teaching Assistant				
Tutor				
Technical Support				
Help Desk				
Librarian				
Counselor				
Graduate Assistant				
Administrator				
Other (specify)				

Check all that apply for individuals' preferences for learning format.

Role of Individual	Preferences											
	On-line Learning (OL)			Face-to-Face Instruction (F2F)			Combination of OL, F2F and Other (Blended)			Other (specify)		
	Yes	No	NA	Yes	No	NA	Yes	No	NA	Yes	No	NA
Learner												
Instructor (full-time)												
Instructor (part-time)												
Teaching Assistant												
Tutor												

Technical Support											
Help Desk											
Librarian											
Counselor											
Graduate Assistant											
Administrator											
Other (specify)											

Content Readiness

Is content ready? (Note: Inventory should specify the location and responsible authors/producers for all multimedia contents, and indicate if permission is needed from copyright holders.)
- ❑ Yes
- ❑ No
- ❑ Not applicable
- ❑ Other (specify)

If *yes*, what percent of content is ready?

Percent (%) Completed	Content Types					
	Text	*Graphics*	*Video*	*Audio*	*Animation*	*Other (specify)*
None						
Less than 50%						
More than 50%						
Other (specify)						

Organization and Change

Check if the institution developed any of the following for its e-learning initiative.
- ❑ Mission Statement
- ❑ Strategic Plan
- ❑ Business Plan
- ❑ Not applicable
- ❑ Other (specify)

To what extent there is buy-in from key players within the institution? Please describe for each key player.

Has the institution made any change in its organizational structure to accommodate the needs of open, flexible, and distributed e-leaning?
- ❑ Yes
- ❑ No
- ❑ Not applicable
- ❑ Other (specify)

If *yes*, please explain below:

Diffusion and Adoption

Does the institution inform the stakeholders (i.e., learners, instructors, support services staff and community members) about the benefits of an e-learning initiative?
- ❑ Yes
- ❑ No
- ❑ Not applicable
- ❑ Other (specify)

Does the institution have a system of keeping all stakeholder groups informed about the activities of its e-learning initiative?
- ❑ Yes
- ❑ No
- ❑ Not applicable
- ❑ Other (specify)

If *yes*, check all that apply:

Stakeholders	Method of Communication (Rate each method from 1-10 scale where 10 represents the most informed and 1 represents the least informed.)				
	E-Mail	*Listserv or Discuss Forum*	*Newsletter*	*Community Newspaper*	*Other (specify)*
Learners					
Instructors					
Support Staff					
Management					
Other (specify)					

Does the institution provide any of the following incentives for any of the following individuals involved in e-learning initiatives?
- ❑ Yes

❑ No
❑ Not applicable
❑ Other (specify)
If *yes*, check all that apply:

Role of Individual	Incentives			
	Release Time	*Financial Reward*	*Tenure*	*Other (specify)*
Instructor				
Trainer				
Teaching Assistant				
Training Assistant				
Tutor				
Project Manager				
Counselor				
Librarian				
Other (specify)				

Implementation

Does the institution clearly identify skills and knowledge required by learners to adopt e-learning?
❑ Yes
❑ No
❑ Not applicable
❑ Other (specify)

Does the institution provide reward or incentives for learners to adopt e-learning?
❑ Yes
❑ No
❑ Not applicable
❑ Other (specify)
If *yes*, please explain below:

Will the key leaders of the institution be involved in day-to-day activities of the e-learning initiative?
❑ Yes
❑ No
❑ Not applicable
❑ Other (specify)

If *yes*, please explain below:
Does the institution's e-learning initiative receive continuing support from key individuals in the institution?
☐ Yes
☐ No
☐ Not applicable
☐ Other (specify)

Budgeting and Return on Investment

Does the institution have a budget for e-learning?
☐ Yes
☐ No
☐ Not applicable
☐ Other (specify)

Check if the institution has budgeted for any of the following costs related to e-learning. Check all that apply:
☐ Content expert
☐ Course designers (i.e., instructional designers)
☐ Computer programmers
☐ Graphic artists
☐ Instructor compensation
☐ Support staff compensation
☐ Consultants
☐ Equipment and software acquisition
☐ Marketing
☐ Delivery
☐ Program revision
☐ Ongoing maintenance and upgrade of equipment and software
☐ Operating costs such as telephone, postage and supplies
☐ Not applicable
☐ Other ((specify)

Formula for Return on Investment (ROI)

$$\text{ROI (\%)} = \frac{\text{Benefits} - \text{Total Costs}}{\text{Total Costs}} \; X \; 100$$

or

$$\text{ROI (\%)} = \frac{\text{Net Benefits}}{\text{Costs}} \; X \; 100$$

Does the institution conduct return on investment (ROI) analysis during any of the following stages of e-learning?
❑ Yes
❑ No
❑ Not applicable
❑ Other (specify)
If *yes*, check all that apply:
   ❑ Before implementation
   ❑ During implementation
   ❑ After implementation
   ❑ Other (specify)

Does the institution put aside any additional money for obtaining any of the following resources that may be needed in the future to continue e-learning?
❑ Yes
❑ No
❑ Not applicable
❑ Other (specify)
If *yes*, check all that apply:
   ❑ Hardware
   ❑ Software
   ❑ Not applicable
   ❑ Other (specify)

Partnership with Other Institutions

Does the institution have partnerships with other e-learning institutions?
❑ Yes
❑ No
❑ Not applicable
❑ Other (specify)
If *yes*, check all that apply:
   ❑ Students can take courses from partner institutions toward a degree
      program
   ❑ Students can transfer courses within partner institutions
   ❑ Not applicable
   ❑ Other (specify)

Can students use library and other learning resources from partner institutions?
❑ Yes
❑ No
❑ Not applicable
❑ Other (specify)

Program and Course Information Catalogue

Check if the institution provides its program and course information via any of the following formats:
❑ Completely on-line
❑ Completely print materials
❑ Partially on-line
❑ Other (please describe)

What is the format of the course?
❑ All on-line
❑ Partially on-line
If partially on-line, what other media are used?
    ❑ Face-to-face classes
    ❑ CD ROMs
    ❑ DVDs
    ❑ Interactive TV
    ❑ Satellite
    ❑ Printed materials
    ❑ Other (please describe)

Are students required to take a prerequisite course before taking an "on-line" course from the institution?
❑ Yes
❑ No
❑ Not applicable
❑ Does not specify
❑ Other (specify)

Is the course a part of a specific degree (or certification) program?
❑ Yes
❑ No
❑ Not applicable
❑ Other (specify)
If *yes*, check all that apply:
    ❑ Required course
    ❑ Elective course
    ❑ Other (please describe)

Does the institution provide information about whether the course can be used toward degree programs in various fields?
❑ Yes

❑ No
❑ Not applicable
❑ Other (specify)

If *yes*, list the name(s) of the academic or professional programs.

Does the course allow students to preview any part of course materials (or course demo) before registration?
❑ Yes
❑ No
❑ Not applicable
❑ Other (specify)

Does the institution provide any information regarding whether the course is transferable to other accredited institutions?
❑ Yes
❑ No
❑ Not applicable
❑ Other (specify)

Does the institution post updated information about the courses that are currently unavailable for registration?
❑ Yes
❑ No
❑ Not applicable
❑ Other (specify)

Does the institution provide information about the accreditation status of the course and the institution?
❑ Yes
❑ No
❑ Not applicable
❑ Other (specify)

Are students required to be part of a degree program to take this course?
❑ Yes
❑ No
❑ Not applicable
❑ Other (specify)

Academic Calendar and Course Schedule

What is the course schedule format?
- ❑ Fixed start and fixed end date
- ❑ Fixed duration (e.g., must be finished within a semester or a year, etc.)
- ❑ Open (can start any time and finish any time)
- ❑ Not applicable
- ❑ Other (specify)

Provide information about the course schedule format:

Quarter / Semester	Year	Course Name	Registration Dates	Course Start Date	Course End Date
Fall					
Winter					
Spring					
Summer					
Other (specify)					

Provide information about the synchronous (or live) activities scheduled for the course:

Live Activities	Date (e.g., May 23, 2004)	Start Time* (e.g., 16:00)	End Time* (e.g., 17:00)
Live Chat			
Audio Conferencing			
Video Conferencing			
Telephone			
Other (specify)			

*UTC (Universal Time Coordinated) which is equivalent to GMT (Greenwich Mean Time) should also be provided for learners located in different time zones.

Check the course duration.
- ❑ Intensive (1-2 months duration)
- ❑ Quarter-based (3 months duration)
- ❑ Semester-based (4 months duration)
- ❑ Independent-study (12 months duration)
- ❑ Self-paced
- ❑ Other (specify)

What is length (i.e., instructional hours) of the course? (Note: The length of the course can be dependent on learners' stated needs or interests. Learners can work on their own paces. For example, they can begin in January and ends in June.)

Tuition and Fees

Does the institution provide information about course tuition and fees?
If *yes*, enter the amount of money in the appropriate boxes below:

Tuition and Fees	Yes	No	NA	US $*
Course Tuition (per credit)				
Technology Fee (per course)				
Registration Processing Fee				
Application Fee for Admission				
Graduation Fee				
Official Transcript				
Graduation Certificate				
Charge for Returned Check				
Other Charges (specify)				

* [If appropriate, use your own currency].

How does *tuition* for on-line students compare to tuition for face-to-face students in the same institution?
❑ Same
❑ Higher
❑ Lower
❑ Not applicable
❑ Other (specify)

Are on-line courses offered at a lower *fee* than on-campus courses? (Note: It is not uncommon for students to expect lower fees for on-line courses since they do not use a physical classroom.)
❑ Yes
❑ No
❑ Not applicable
❑ Other (specify)

How does *tuition* compare to that of *similar institutions*?
❑ Same
❑ Higher
❑ Lower

❑ Not applicable
❑ Other (specify)

How do *fees* compare to those of *similar institutions*?
❑ Same
❑ Higher
❑ Lower
❑ Not applicable
❑ Other (specify)

How does *tuition* compare to that of *partner institutions*?
❑ Same
❑ Higher
❑ Lower
❑ Not applicable
❑ Other (specify)

How do *fees* compare to that of *partner institutions*?
❑ Same
❑ Higher
❑ Lower
❑ Not applicable
❑ Other (specify)

Does the institution provide a Withdrawal Request Form (WRF) on-line?
❑ Yes
❑ No
❑ Not applicable
❑ Other (specify)
If *yes*, check all that apply:
    ❑ Students can submit WRF On-line
    ❑ Students can fax WRF
    ❑ Students can send WRF via regular mail
    ❑ Other (specify)

Does the course provide clear information about refund policies?
❑ Yes
❑ No
❑ Not applicable
❑ Other (specify)
If *yes*, enter % of reimbursement of tuition in the appropriate places below:

Withdrawal Date	Percentage of Tuition Refunded
1st Week	
2nd Week	

3rd Week	
4th Week	
5th Week	
6th Week	
Other (specify)	

May the institution change fees without notice?
- ❑ Yes
- ❑ No
- ❑ Not applicable
- ❑ Other (specify)

Marketing and Recruitment

Does the institution offer information sessions to recruit students?
- ❑ Yes
- ❑ No
- ❑ Not applicable
- ❑ Other (specify)

If *yes*, check all the apply:
- ❑ On-line information session
- ❑ Face-to-face information sessions
- ❑ Not applicable
- ❑ Other (specify)

Check if the institution has any of the following for its e-learning marketing team.
Check all the apply:
- ❑ Market researcher
- ❑ Recruiter
- ❑ Not applicable
- ❑ Other (specify)

Does the course offer features (e.g., attractive design, quick loading time, comprehensive content, multi-cultural, etc.) that make it highly marketable?
- ❑ Yes
- ❑ No
- ❑ Not applicable
- ❑ Other (specify)

Does the institution market its e-learning offerings?
- ❑ Yes
- ❑ No
- ❑ Not applicable

❑ Other (specify)

If *yes*, indicate if the institution uses any of the following means to market its e-learning offerings. Check all the apply:

- ❑ Websites
- ❑ Internet banner ads
- ❑ E-mail
- ❑ Listserv postings
- ❑ Newsletter
- ❑ Newspaper
- ❑ Magazine
- ❑ Journal
- ❑ Radio
- ❑ TV
- ❑ Posters
- ❑ Free promotional gifts
- ❑ No applicable
- ❑ Other (specify)

Does the institution provide previous students' testimonials about its e-learning courses and programs?

- ❑ Yes
- ❑ No
- ❑ Not applicable
- ❑ Other (specify)

Does the institution provide information about student attrition (or dropout) rate? (Note: Institutions need a process and a person responsible for analyzing attrition and creating strategies to reduce it.)

- ❑ Yes
- ❑ No
- ❑ Not applicable
- ❑ Other (specify)

Does the institution provide any statistics on how many students successfully completed the on-line course?

- ❑ Yes
- ❑ No
- ❑ Not applicable
- ❑ Other (specify)

Does the institution provide any statistics on the types of barriers causing attrition?

- ❑ Yes
- ❑ No
- ❑ Not applicable

❑ Other (specify)

If *yes*, enter % dropped due to each barrier in the appropriate boxes below:

Barriers	Percent (%) Dropped for the Barrier
Lack of free time	
Change in circumstances	
Took more time than expected	
Personal study problems	
Unclear goals	
Time management problems	
Problem with course schedule and pacing	
Learning materials arrive late	
Insufficient feedback on assignments	
Insufficient/unsatisfactory communication with instructional staff	
Course focus and expectations not clear	
Inflexible course structure	
Course content outdated	
Confusing changes to course	
Unresponsive instructor	
Inadequate technical support	
Inadequate library support	
Difficult content	
Mismatch in assessment requirement	
Course focus lacked personal relevance or interest	
Lacked prerequisite knowledge	
Other (specify)	

Admissions

Does the institution provide admission requirements information on-line?
❑ Yes
❑ No
❑ Not applicable
❑ Other (specify)

Do students have access to individual(s) at the admission office?
❑ Yes
❑ No
❑ Not applicable

❑ Other (specify)
If *yes*, indicate the means of communication (check all that apply):
    ❑ Phone
    ❑ E-mail
    ❑ On-line (realtime)
    ❑ Other (specify)

Does the institution provide information about transfer credit requirements?
❑ Yes
❑ No
❑ Not applicable
❑ Other (specify)

Check if students can submit Admission Application Form via any of the
following methods. Check all that apply:
❑ On-line
❑ Regular mail
❑ Other (specify)

Can students submit all required admission forms on-line?
❑ Yes
❑ No
❑ Not applicable
❑ Other (specify)

Can students inquire about the status of their application on-line?
❑ Yes
❑ No
❑ Not applicable
❑ Other (specify)

Financial Aid

Can students apply for financial aid on-line?
❑ Yes
❑ No
❑ Not applicable
❑ Other (specify)

Are students informed about how soon they receive financial aid eligibility?
❑ Yes
❑ No
❑ Not applicable

❑ Other (specify)

Do on-line students receive the same financial aid programs as on-campus students?
❑ Yes
❑ No, they do not receive any financial aid
❑ No, they have special financial aid programs
❑ Not applicable
❑ Other (specify)

Does the institution offer federal work-study or community service opportunities for on-line students?
❑ Yes
❑ No
❑ Not applicable
❑ Other (specify)

Does the institution have any scholarships available for on-line students?
❑ Yes
❑ No
❑ Not applicable
❑ Other (specify)

Does the institution provide links to scholarship Websites? (Note: In the USA, sites such as http://www.wiredscholar.com provide scholarship information based on location, age, school year, and heritage of applicants.)
❑ Yes
❑ No
❑ Not applicable
❑ Other (specify)

Registration and Payment

Can students register on-line?
❑ Yes
❑ No
❑ Not applicable
❑ Other (specify)
If *no*, check other type(s) of registration methods available for the course:
  ❑ By regular mail
  ❑ By telephone call to a person doing registration
  ❑ By fax
  ❑ By touch-tone phone

❑ Other (specify)

Does the institution have an on-line system that gives students a secure method of making their tuition and fees payment?
❑ Yes
❑ No
❑ Not applicable

How do students pay tuition and fees? (Check all that apply):

Methods of Payment (Tuition and Fees)	Transaction	
	On-line	*Off-line*
Credit cards		
Checks		
Electronic money transfer		
Money order		
Electronic checks (e.g., Western Union in the USA)		
Automatic debit system		
Gift certificates or coupons		
Other (specify)		

If registration is done on-line, does the student receive confirmation of registration?
   ❑ Yes
   ❑ No
   ❑ Not applicable
   If *yes*, check all that apply:
      ❑ Confirmation receives on-line (e.g., e-mail, on-line message, etc.)
      ❑ Confirmation receives off-line (e.g., letter, phone, etc.)
      ❑ Other (specify)

Does the institution have a system for providing on-line billing information?
❑ Yes
❑ No
❑ Not applicable
❑ Other (specify)

Does the institution provide on-line procedures for dropping or withdrawing from an e-learning course?
❑ Yes
❑ No
❑ Not applicable
❑ Other (specify)
If *yes*, is any penalty involved?
   ❑ Yes

❑ No
❑ Not applicable
❑ Other (specify)

If the course is offered in modules at different times, does the institution allow students the flexibility to enroll for their desired module(s)?
❑ Yes
❑ No
❑ Not applicable
❑ Other (specify)

Would student information submitted on-line to the registrar's office be kept secure and confidential to the extent possible?
❑ Yes
❑ No
❑ Not applicable

Does the institution provide enrollment history of the course (i.e., how many students enrolled in the course in past semesters)?
❑ Yes
❑ No
❑ Not applicable
❑ Other (specify)

Does the institution provide the completion history of the course (i.e., what percent of enrolled students completed the course)?
❑ Yes
❑ No
❑ Not applicable
❑ Other (specify)

Does the course offer a money-back guarantee?
❑ Yes
❑ No
❑ Not applicable
❑ Other (specify)

Is the following registration-related information for the course provided?
❑ Total number of seats allocated for the course
❑ Number of seats available
❑ Not applicable
❑ Other (specify)

Information Technology Services

Do students have any of the following facilities or support from the information technology services?
- ❏ Yes
- ❏ No
- ❏ Not applicable
- ❏ Other (specify)

If *yes*, check all the apply:
- ❏ Borrow a laptop
- ❏ Borrow a PDA (Personal Digital Assistant)
- ❏ Borrow technical computer books/manuals
- ❏ Borrow a scanner
- ❏ Borrow a digital camera
- ❏ Borrow a video camera
- ❏ Borrow a digital video camera
- ❏ Borrow an e-book reader
- ❏ Borrow software
- ❏ Receive spaces on the servers for personal Web pages
- ❏ Receive e-mail account
- ❏ Technical support
- ❏ Help desk
- ❏ Not applicable
- ❏ Other (specify)

Is the institution's information technology or computing services department involved in the selection of a learning management system (LMS) and/or learning content management system (LCMS) for e-learning?
- ❏ Yes
- ❏ No
- ❏ Not applicable
- ❏ Other (specify)

If *yes*, check if inputs from any of the following are considered in the LMS and LCMS selection process. Check all the apply:
- ❏ Instructional designers
- ❏ Content expert
- ❏ Instructors
- ❏ Students
- ❏ Technical support staff
- ❏ Library support staff
- ❏ Help desk
- ❏ Other (specify)

Instructional Design and Media Services

Does the institution have any of the following individuals involved in the creation of e-learning materials?
- ❑ Yes
- ❑ No
- ❑ Not applicable

If *yes*, check all the apply:
- ❑ Content or subject matter expert
- ❑ Instructional designer
- ❑ Programmer
- ❑ Multimedia designers
- ❑ Graphic artists
- ❑ Not applicable
- ❑ Other (specify)

Graduation

Does the institution provide an on-line means for tracking course completion in a program of study?
- ❑ Yes
- ❑ No
- ❑ Not applicable
- ❑ Other (specify)

Does the institution provide graduation information on-line?
- ❑ Yes
- ❑ No
- ❑ Not applicable
- ❑ Other (specify)

Does the institution update students about whether they completed all required courses toward a degree or not?
- ❑ Yes
- ❑ No
- ❑ Not applicable
- ❑ Other (specify)

Can students check the completion status of each course in their program plans before completing Graduation Application Form?
- ❑ Yes
- ❑ No

❑ Not applicable
❑ Other (specify)
If *yes*, check all that apply:
   ❑ Students can access their program plans on-line
   ❑ Students can call the admissions office to check the status of their program plan
   ❑ Admission or graduation office can e-mail their latest program plan to students
   ❑ Admission or graduation office can mail their latest program plan to students
   ❑ Other (specify)

Does the institution provide Graduation Application Form (GAF) on-line?
❑ Yes
❑ No
❑ Not applicable
❑ Other (specify)
If *yes*, check all that apply:
   ❑ Students can submit the GAF On-line
   ❑ Students can fax the GAF
   ❑ Students can send the GAF via regular mail
   ❑ Other (specify)

Does the institution host a graduation ceremony for students who complete their programs totally on-line?
❑ Yes
❑ No
❑ Not applicable
❑ Other (specify)
If *yes*, check all that apply:
   ❑ Cyber Graduation Ceremony
   ❑ Onsite Graduation at the campus
   ❑ Other (specify)

Does the institution provide a Certificate Request Form (CRF) on-line?
❑ Yes
❑ No
❑ Not applicable
❑ Other (specify)
If *yes*, check all that apply:
   ❑ Students can submit a CRF on-line
   ❑ Students can fax a CRF
   ❑ Students can send a CRF via regular mail
   ❑ Other (specify)

Transcripts and Grades

Does the course provide the date for reporting the final grade?
- ❑ Yes
- ❑ No
- ❑ Not applicable
- ❑ Other (specify)

Does the course provide students' grades on-line?
- ❑ Yes
- ❑ No
- ❑ Not applicable

If *yes*, check all that apply:
- ❑ Weekly grading summary
- ❑ Mid-term grading summary
- ❑ Final grading summary
- ❑ Other (specify)

Does the institution provide a Transcript Request Form (TRF) on-line?
- ❑ Yes
- ❑ No
- ❑ Not applicable

If *yes*, check all that apply:
- ❑ Students can submit a TRF on-line
- ❑ Students can fax a TRF
- ❑ Students can send a TRF via regular mail
- ❑ Other (specify)

Does the institution provide information about the costs for official transcripts?
- ❑ Yes
- ❑ No
- ❑ Not applicable

If *yes*, enter the costs for official transcripts in the appropriate boxes:

Transcript Delivery	Cost per Transcript (within the country)	Cost per Transcript (outside the country)
Regular Mail		
Fax		
24-hour Mail		
48-hour Mail		
Other (specify)		

Accreditation

Is the institution accredited?
- ❏ Yes
- ❏ No
- ❏ Not applicable
- ❏ Other (specify)

If *yes*, indicate the name of the accrediting agency:

If *no*, check all that apply:
- ❏ Never applied for accreditation
- ❏ Application Pending
- ❏ Previously denied, applied again
- ❏ Other (specify)

Policies

Does the institution have e-learning policies and guidelines?
- ❏ Yes
- ❏ No
- ❏ Not applicable
- ❏ Other (specify)

Instructional Quality

Does the institution provide a list of mentors and/or tutors who are available to assist on-line students?
- ❏ Yes
- ❏ No
- ❏ Not applicable
- ❏ Other (specify)

Does the instructional staff maintain scheduled office hours for students?
- ❏ Yes
- ❏ No
- ❏ Not applicable
- ❏ Other (specify)

If yes, check the number of hours *per week*:

Instructional Staff	Hours /Week				
	5	10	15	20	Other
Instructor					
Tutor					
Other (specify)					

Check if students can contact instructional staff using any of the following methods during the posted office hours. Check all that apply:

Instructional Staff	Communication Methods					
	Phone	E-mail	Chat Room	Audio Conferencing	Video Conferencing	Other
Instructor						
Tutor						
Other (specify)						

Does the instructor check with students at the beginning and during the on-line course whether they are comfortable using on-line technologies for the course? (Note: The instructor cannot take for granted that all students who attended the course orientation know how to use all the required technological tasks in the course).
❑ Yes
❑ No
❑ Not applicable
❑ Other (specify)

Does the course provide academic quality such as one would expect in a traditional course?
❑ Yes
❑ No
❑ Not applicable
❑ Other (specify)

If an emergency arises for the instructor, does the course employ a substitute instructor so that students' learning is not interrupted?
❑ Yes
❑ No
❑ Not applicable
❑ Other (specify)

Does the instructor foster an environment of open communication where students can feel comfortable sharing their opinions?
❑ Yes
❑ No
❑ Not applicable

❑ Other (specify)

How soon does the instructor return students' telephone calls?
❑ Within 24 hours
❑ Within 48 hours
❑ Within 72 hours
❑ Within a week
❑ Not applicable
❑ Other (specify)

How soon does the instructor reply to students' e-mail questions?
❑ Within 24 hours
❑ Within 48 hours
❑ Within 72 hours
❑ Within a week
❑ Not applicable
❑ Other (specify)

When e-mail communication is not enough or adequate in clarifying or discussing sensitive issues, are any of the following options available?
❑ Yes
❑ No
❑ Not applicable
❑ Other (specify)
If *yes*, check all that apply:
    ❑ The instructor calls students
    ❑ Students can call instructor
    ❑ Other (specify)
    ❑ Not applicable

Is the "content expert" who originally designed the course actually teaching the course?
❑ Yes
❑ No
❑ Not applicable
❑ Other (specify)

Is there a "faculty forum" where geographically dispersed faculty members can communicate and exchange ideas to improve their on-line teaching?
❑ Yes
❑ No
❑ Not applicable
❑ Other (specify)

Is there someone in the institution who compares the accuracy of the course description in the course syllabus with the actual description of the course approved by the curriculum committee?

❑ Yes
❑ No
❑ Not applicable
❑ Other (specify)

Faculty and Staff Support

Check if any of the following have experience teaching on-line courses.

Role of Individual	Yes	No	NA	Unknown	Other (specify)
Instructor (full-time)					
Instructor (part-time)					
Teaching Assistant					
Tutor					
Technical Support					
Librarian					
Counselor					
Graduate Assistant					
E-Learning Administrator					
Other (specify)					

Check if any of the following have experience as on-line students themselves.

Role of Individual	Yes	No	NA	Unknown	Other (specify)
Instructor (full-time)					
Instructor (part-time)					
Teaching Assistant					
Tutor					
Technical Support					
Librarian					
Counselor					
Graduate Assistant					
E-Learning Administrator					
Other (specify)					

Check if any of the following receive adequate training to use computer and Internet technologies comfortably to teach/support on-line courses via any of the following delivery methods.

Role of Individual	Delivery Medium					
	On-line	*Face-to-Face*	*Printed Manual*	*Training CDs*	*Blended (Mixture of on-line, f2f, print, CDs, etc.)*	*Other (specify)*
Instructor (full-time)						
Instructor (part-time)						
Teaching Assistant						
Tutor						
Technical Support						
Librarian						
Counselor						
Graduate Assistant						
E-Learning Administrator						
Other (specify)						

Check if any of the following individuals receive training on the *learning management system* (LMS) and/or the *learning content management system* (LCMS) via any of the following delivery methods. (For example, at the University of Maryland University College, students can take the Online Test Drive for WebTycho, the learning management system used in their on-line courses (http://umuc.edu/distance/de_orien/testdrv_frm.html).

Role of Individual	Delivery Medium										
	On-line		*Face-to-Face*		*Printed Manual*		*Training CDs*		*Blended (Mixture of on-line, f2f, print, CDs, etc.)*		*Other (specify)*
	LMS	LCMS	LMS	LCMS	LMS	LCMS	LMS	LCMS	LMS	LCMS	
Instructor (full-time)											
Instructor (part-time)											

Teaching Assistant						
Tutor						
Technical Support						
Graduate Assistant						
Other (specify)						

Check if any of the following individuals receive training on *moderating on-line discussions* via any of the following delivery methods?

Role of Individual	Delivery Medium					
	On-line	*Face-to-Face*	*Printed Manual*	*Training CDs*	*Blended (Mixture of on-line, f2f, print, CDs, etc.)*	*Other (specify)*
Instructor (full-time)						
Instructor (part-time)						
Teaching Assistant						
Tutor						
Graduate Assistant						
Counselor						
Technical Support						
Other (specify)						

Do new faculty (first time teaching on-line) get technical help to set up their courses?
- ❑ Yes
- ❑ No
- ❑ Not applicable
- ❑ Other (specify)

Are mentors assigned to new faculty (first time teaching on-line)?
- ❑ Yes
- ❑ No
- ❑ Not applicable
- ❑ Other (specify)

Do mentors monitor or observe new faculty throughout the semester and provide feedback for improvement?
- ❑ Yes
- ❑ No
- ❑ Not applicable
- ❑ Other (specify)

Does the institution have a program or initiative to motivate any of the following instructional and support staff to devote more time and effort in facilitating students' learning? (Note: On-line teaching demands more time and effort from instructional staff. Sometimes they have to go out of their way to help learners. If they are not paid for their extra efforts, they may not be motivated to go the extra mile to provide their services.)
- ❑ Yes
- ❑ No
- ❑ Not applicable
- ❑ Other (specify)

If *yes*, check all that apply:

Instructional and Support Staff	Yes	No	NA	Unknown	Other (specify)
Instructor (full-time)					
Instructor (part-time)					
Teaching Assistant					
Tutor					
Technical Support					
Librarian					
Counselor					
Graduate Assistant					
E-Learning Administrator					
Other (specify)					

Does the instructional staff (e.g., instructor, trainer, and tutor) have adequate computers and connections systems to teach on-line courses?
- ❑ Yes
- ❑ No
- ❑ Not applicable
- ❑ Other (specify)

Does the technical support staff have adequate computers and connections systems to support on-line courses?
- ❑ Yes
- ❑ No
- ❑ Not applicable

❑ Other (specify)

Does the other staff (e.g., librarian, counselor) have adequate computers and connections systems to support on-line courses?
❑ Yes
❑ No
❑ Not applicable
❑ Other (specify)

In on-line learning, the instructor plays the roles of a facilitator, mentor and coach. Does the instructor receive training on how to play these roles?
❑ Yes
❑ No
❑ Not applicable
❑ Other (specify)

Does the instructor receive adequate training on the software used in the course in order to answer students' questions or direct them to the appropriate help desk?
❑ Yes
❑ No
❑ Not applicable
❑ Other (specify)

Do technical and other staff receive training on how to communicate with remote learners in difficult situations?
❑ Yes
❑ No
❑ Not applicable
❑ Other (specify)

Does the institution provide any of the following handbooks?
❑ Yes
❑ No
❑ Not applicable
❑ Other (specify)
If *yes*, check all that apply:
    ❑ Student handbook
    ❑ Faculty handbook
    ❑ Tutor handbook
    ❑ Technical support staff handbook
    ❑ Other support services staff handbook
    ❑ E-Learning administrator handbook
    ❑ Other (specify)
    ❑ Not applicable

Does the institution provide faculty development courses on-line? (For example, Capella University provides Faculty Development Courses and Seminars (http://Capella.edu/aspscripts/centers/faculty/resources/fcforms.asp).
❑ Yes
❑ No
❑ Not applicable
❑ Other (specify)

Does the institution provide on-line seminars for faculty and staff on on-line learning issues?
❑ Yes
❑ No
❑ Not applicable
❑ Other (specify)

Workload, Class Size, and Compensation

Does the institution have a rewards system to recognize the type of dedication faculty members make in teaching on-line courses?
❑ Yes
❑ No
❑ Not applicable
❑ Other (specify)

Does the institution provide any kind of compensation, benefits, or rewards to staff who take on-line training or staff development courses on their own time (not during their work hours)?
❑ Yes
❑ No
❑ Not applicable
❑ Other (specify)
If yes, describe the types of compensations, benefits or rewards.

Does the instructor receive any of the following from the institution as incentives for creating e-learning?
❑ Yes
❑ No
❑ Not applicable
❑ Other (specify)
If *yes*, check the range below:
    ❑ Release time
    ❑ Travel funds to conference
    ❑ Course development funds

❑ Encouragement from peers
❑ Encouragement from administrators
❑ Not applicable
❑ Other (specify)

Does the course limit the number of students per instructor?
❑ Yes
❑ No
❑ Not applicable
❑ Other (specify)
If *yes*, check the range below:

☐ 10 - 20	☐ 20 - 30	☐ 30 - 40	☐ 40 - 50	☐ 50 - 60
☐ 60- 70	☐ 70 - 80	☐ 80 - 90	☐ 90 - 100	☐ 100 - 110
☐ No limit	☐ Not sure	☐ NA	☐ Other (specify)	

Does the course limit the number of students per tutor?
❑ Yes
❑ No
❑ Not applicable
❑ Other (specify)
If *yes*, check the range below:

☐ 10 - 20	☐ 20 - 30	☐ 30 - 40	☐ 40 - 50	☐ 50 - 60
☐ 60- 70	☐ 70 - 80	☐ 80 - 90	☐ 90 - 100	☐ 100 - 110
☐ No limit	☐ Not sure	☐ NA	☐ Other (specify)	

Intellectual Property Rights

Does the institution have clear e-learning related policies on the following issues?
❑ Workload and compensation
❑ Intellectual property rights
❑ Not applicable
❑ Other (specify)

Who owns the rights to the materials on the course Website?
❑ Instructor
❑ Content or subject matter expert
❑ Institution
❑ Not applicable
❑ Other (specify)

Do faculty members take course content with them when they leave the
institution?
❑ Yes
❑ No

❑ Not applicable
❑ Other (specify)

Pre-enrollment Services

Are students expected to complete a general and demographic information survey? (Check appropriate option)
❑ Yes, because it is required by institution
❑ Yes, because it is recommended by institution
❑ No
❑ Not applicable
❑ Other (specify)

Does the institution provide contact information of some former students of the course whom new students can contact to get students' perspective of the course? (Note: In traditional on-campus courses students can find former students to get more information about the course and instructor before registration).
❑ Yes
❑ No
❑ Not applicable
❑ Other (specify)

Does the course make previous students' course evaluations available to potential new students?
❑ Yes
❑ No
❑ Not applicable
❑ Other (specify)

Orientation

Check if any of the following individuals are available during on-line orientation.

Instructional and Support Staff	Yes	No	NA	Other (specify)
Instructor (full-time)				
Instructor (part-time)				

Teaching Assistant				
Tutor				
Technical Support				
Librarian				
Counselor				
Graduate Assistant				
E-Learning Administrator				
Other (specify)				

Do students receive any guidelines on how to interact effectively on-line?
- ❑ Yes
- ❑ No
- ❑ Not applicable
- ❑ Other (specify)

Do students receive training on browser skills?
- ❑ Yes
- ❑ No
- ❑ Not applicable
- ❑ Other (specify)

Are students informed about any of the following technical skills that they can use to become successful in on-line learning?
- ❑ Yes
- ❑ No
- ❑ Not applicable
- ❑ Other (specify)

If *yes*, check all that apply:
- ❑ Students can open both a word processor and browser at the same
- ❑ Students can take notes in a word processor while using the course browser
- ❑ Other (specify)

Are there any tips provided during the orientation that can help students to become successful in on-line learning?
- ❑ Yes
- ❑ No
- ❑ Not applicable
- ❑ Other (specify)

Does the institution provide a student handbook or other guide that contains important information about relevant institutional policies and procedures?
- ❑ Yes
- ❑ No
- ❑ Not applicable

❑ Other (specify)
If *yes*, check all that apply:
    ❑ It is available on-line
    ❑ It is mailed to students before orientation
    ❑ It is mailed to students after orientation
    ❑ Other (specify)

Are students required to post their biographies?
❑ Yes
❑ No
❑ Not applicable
❑ Other (specify)
If *yes*, can any of the following be included with the biography? Check all that apply:
    ❑ Photographs
    ❑ E-mail addresses
    ❑ Video clips
    ❑ Audio clips
    ❑ Other (specify below)

Does the instructor read and reply to students' biographies when appropriate (as a symbol of a warm welcome)?
❑ Yes
❑ No
❑ Not applicable
❑ Other (specify)

Does the course provide a self-test to check students' understanding of orientation and course materials?
❑ Yes
❑ No
❑ Not applicable
❑ Other (specify)

Does the institution provide an ID cards to individuals involved in e-learning?
❑ Yes
❑ No
❑ Not applicable
❑ Other (specify)

Check if any of the following individuals receive ID cards from the institution.

Role of Individual	Yes	No	NA	Other (specify)
Distance students				

Distance instructors				
Distance Teaching Assistants				
Distance Tutors				
Other (specify)				

Does the institution provide 'I.D. Card Request' form on-line?
☐ Yes
☐ No
☐ Not applicable
☐ Other (specify)

How do distance students and staff apply for ID cards? Check all that apply:
☐ Submit their signed and completed I.D. Card Request forms at the campus Registrar's Office where their pictures are taken.
☐ They can mail their signed and completed I.D. Card Request forms with their passport sized photos (signed in the back) to the Registrar's Office.
☐ They can e-mail their completed I.D. Card Request forms with their digital photos and scanned copy of the drivers' licenses, passport pages (JPEG or GIF file) or any documents showing their identities to the Registrar's Office.
☐ Not applicable
☐ Other (specify)

Faculty and Staff Directories

Does the institution provide faculty and staff directories on-line?
☐ Yes
☐ No
☐ Not applicable
☐ Other (specify)
If *yes*, check all that are available in the directories:
  ☐ E-mail address
  ☐ Telephone number
  ☐ Fax number
  ☐ Home page
  ☐ Mailing address
  ☐ Other (specify)

Advising

Does the institution provide academic and enrollment advising?
☐ Yes

❑ No
❑ Not applicable
❑ Other (specify)
If *yes*, check all that apply:

Communication Mode	Advising Issues						
	Application Forms	*Transcript Review*	*Course Selection*	*Transfer Credits*	*Degree Program Plan*	*Graduation Forms*	*Other (specify)*
E-mail							
On campus in-person meetings							
Advisors travel to remote sites							
Chat rooms							
Instant messaging							
Bulletin board							
Listserv							
FAQs							
Phone							
Toll-free telephone							
Audio conferencing							
Video conferencing							
Fax							
Regular mail							
Promotional materials							
Admission packets							
Pre-enrollment Materials							
Other (specify)							

Check if any of the following provide academic advising?

Advising by	Yes (check hours)			No	NA	Other (specify)
	Hours Per Week					
	1 - 5	*6 - 10*	*Other*			
Instructor (full-time)						
Instructor (part-time)						

Teaching Assistant						
Tutor						
Former Students (Paid)						
Former Students (Volunteer)						
Other (specify)						

Is there a "peer-guide" system available for new students to get guidance from existing students who have completed one or more courses in e-learning?
- ❑ Yes
- ❑ No
- ❑ Not applicable
- ❑ Other (specify)

Learning Skills Development

Does the course provide a learner's guide?
- ❑ Yes, available online
- ❑ Yes, available in print
- ❑ No
- ❑ Not applicable
- ❑ Other (specify)

Services for Students with Disabilities

Check if the institution provides special services for any of the following types of disabilities. Check all that apply:
- ❑ Visual impairments (blind or impaired sight)
- ❑ Hearing impairments (deaf or hard of hearing)
- ❑ Speech impairments
- ❑ Mobility impairments (restricted manual skills)
- ❑ Dyslexic
- ❑ Mental health difficulties
- ❑ Medical conditions
- ❑ Other learning difficulties (specify)

Bookstore

Does the institution have an on-line bookstore?

❑ Yes
❑ No
❑ Not applicable

If *yes*, can students purchase textbooks and packages of course-related supplemental reading materials on-line from the campus bookstore?

    ❑ Yes
    ❑ No
    ❑ Not applicable
    ❑ Other (specify)

Does the campus bookstore ship texts and packages of course-related supplemental reading materials to students?

❑ Yes
❑ No
❑ Not applicable
❑ Other (specify)

Does the institution provide links to on-line bookstores where the students can purchase their textbooks?

❑ Yes
❑ No
❑ Not applicable
❑ Other (specify)

Does the institution have a developed partnership with an on-line bookstore where the students can purchase their textbooks with a discount?

❑ Yes
❑ No
❑ Not applicable
❑ Other (specify)

Tutorial Services

Does the institution provide tutorial services?

❑ Yes
❑ No
❑ Not applicable
❑ Other (specify)

Does the instructor (or academic advisor) monitor students' performance during the course?

❑ Yes
❑ No

❑ Not applicable
❑ Other (specify)
If *yes*, check all that apply:
    ❑ Struggling students are advised to use the tutorial services provided by the institution
    ❑ Other (specify)

Mediation and Conflict Resolution

Does the institution have a system to accept students' complaints via any of the following?
❑ Yes
❑ No
❑ Not applicable
If *yes*, check all that apply:
    ❑ Telephone
    ❑ On-line drop box
    ❑ E-mail
    ❑ Regular mail
    ❑ Other (specify)

Does the institution have an Ombuds Office which students can contact for any of following?
❑ Yes
❑ No
❑ Not applicable
If *yes*, check all that apply:
    ❑ Academic grievances
    ❑ Grade disputes
    ❑ Student/instructor conflicts
    ❑ Sexual harassment
    ❑ Discrimination concerns
    ❑ Other (specify)

Student Newsletter

Does the institution have a student newsletter?
❑ Yes
❑ No
❑ Not applicable
❑ Other (specify)

If *yes*, check all that apply:

Newsletter Type	Delivery Format			
	E-mail	Web-based	Print-based	Other (specify)
Daily newsletter				
Weekly newsletter				
Monthly newsletter				
Quarterly newsletter				
Semesterly newsletter				
Other (specify)				

Internship and Employment Services

Check if the institution provides any of the following internship and employment services to students?

Information and Services	Internship	Employment	Other
Information about full-time positions			
Information about part-time positions			
Counseling services			
Other (specify)			

Alumni Affairs

Does the institution have an alumni association?
❑ Yes
❑ No
❑ Not applicable
❑ Other (specify)
If *yes*, check all that are available:
    ❑ Alumni Discussion Forum
    ❑ Directory of Alumni
    ❑ Other (specify)

MANAGEMENT

People

Underline the roles and responsibilities of individuals listed in the "Responsibilities" column of the table below. Also, add any additional duties in the blank spaces.

Role of Individual	Responsibilities
Director	Directs e-learning initiatives. Develops e-learning plans and strategies.
Project Manager	Supervises the overall e-learning process including: design, production, delivery, evaluation, budgeting, staffing and scheduling. Works with coordinators of various e-learning teams.
Business Developer	Develops business plan, marketing plan, and promotion plan. Coordinates internal and external strategic partnerships.
Consultant / Advisor	Provides independent, expert advice and services during various stages of e-learning.
	Content Development Process
Research and Design Coordinator	Coordinates e-learning research and design processes. Informs management and design teams about the latest data pertaining to online learning activities and research.
Content or Subject Matter Expert	Writes course content and reviews existing course materials (if any) for accuracy and currency.
Instructional Designer	Provides consultation on instructional strategies and techniques for e-learning contents and resources. Helps select delivery format and assessment strategies for e-learning.
Interface Designer	Responsible for site design, navigation, accessibility and usability testing. Responsible for reviewing interface design and content materials to be compliant with the accessibility guidelines (e.g., section 508 of American disability Act - ADA).
Copyright Coordinator	Provides advice on intellectual property issues relevant to e-learning. Responsible for negotiating permission to use copyrighted materials including articles, books chapters, videos, music, animations, graphics,

	Web pages, etc. from copyright holders.
Evaluation Specialist	Responsible for evaluation and assessment design and methodology. Conducts and manages student assessment and evaluation of e-learning environments.
Production Coordinator	Coordinates e-learning production process.
Course Integrator	Responsible for getting all pieces of e-learning (e.g., Web pages, chat rooms, Java applets, e-commerce, etc.) working together under a learning management system.
Programmer	Programs e-learning lessons following the storyboard created in the design process.
Editor	Reviews e-learning materials for clarity, consistency of style, grammar, spelling, appropriate references and copyright information.
Graphic Artist	Uses creativity and style to design graphical images for e-learning lessons.
Multimedia Developer	Responsible for creating multimedia learning objects such as audio, video, 2D/3D animations, simulations, etc.
Photographer/ Videographer (cameraman)	Responsible for photography and video related to e-learning contents.
Learning Objects Specialist	Guides the design, production and meaningful storage of learning objects by following internationally recognized standards (e.g., SCORM, AICC, IEEE, etc.).
Quality Assurance	Responsible for quality control in e-learning.
Pilot Subjects	Participants in e-learning pilot testing.
	Content Delivery and Maintenance Process
Delivery Coordinator	Coordinates the implementation of e-learning courses and resources.
Systems	Administers LMS server, user accounts and network security.

Administrator	
Server/Database Programmer	Responsible for server and database related programming especially for tracking and recording learners' activities.
Online Course Coordinator	Coordinates the instructional and support staff for online courses.
Instructor (or Trainer)	Teaches online courses.
Instructor Assistant	Assists the instructor or trainer in instruction.
Tutor	Assists learners in learning tasks.
Discussion Facilitator or Moderator	Moderates and facilitates online discussions.
Customer Service	Provides generic help and points to appropriate support services based on specific needs of customers (i.e., learners).
Technical Support Specialist	Provides both hardware and software related technical help.
Library Services	Interactive library services for learners who can ask questions to librarians about their research both asynchronously and in real time via the Internet.
Counseling Services	Provides guidance on study skills, self-discipline, responsibility for own learning, time management and stress management, etc.
Administrative Services	Administrative services include admissions, schedules, etc.
Registration Services	Responsible for efficient and secure registration process for e-learning.
Marketing	Responsible for marketing e-learning offerings.
Other (specify)	

Management Team

Check the skill level of the management team. (check all that apply):

Skill Types	Management Team														
	Director					Project Manager					Other (specify)				
	Excellent	Good	Fair	Poor	NA	Excellent	Good	Fair	Poor	NA	Excellent	Good	Fair	Poor	NA
Recruiting															
Supervising															
Budgeting															
Planning															
Scheduling															
Assigning tasks to team members															
Interpersonal															
Presentation															
Technological															
Research															
Outsourcing projects components															
Tracking Project Progress															
Conducting Meetings															
Oral Communication															
Written Communication															
Consensus Building															
Conflict Resolution															
Ability to work with others on a team															
Other (specify)															
Other (specify)															
Other (specify)															

Are the budgets maintained efficiently to keep e-learning updated and running without any financial problems?

❑ Yes
❑ No
❑ Not applicable

List various e-learning skills acquired by individuals within the institution (for an example, Mr. Lee's skills are listed in the table below):

Name of the Person	E-Learning Skills
Lee	Taught online courses. Instructional design and programming skills

Identify person ideal for roles and responsibilities during e-learning process.
Check all that apply:

Name	Director	Project Manager	Business Developer	Consultant / Advisor	Other (specify)	Design Coordinator	Content or Subject Matter Expert	Instructional Designer	Interface Designer	Copyright Coordinator	Evaluation Specialist	Other (specify)	Production Coordinator	Course Integrator	Programmer	Graphic Artist	Multimedia Developer	Editor	Learning Objects Specialist	Quality Assurance	Other (specify)	Evaluation Specialist	Instructional Designer	Interface Designer	Other (e.g., Pilot Subjects)	Delivery Coordinator	Systems Administrator	Server/Database Programmer	Other (specify)

Identify outside contractor (i.e., outsourcing) ideal for roles and responsibilities during e-learning process. Check all that apply:

Name	Director	Project Manager	Business Developer	Consultant / Advisor	Other (specify)	Design Coordinator	Content or Subject Matter Expert	Instructional Designer	Interface Designer	Copyright Coordinator	Evaluation Specialist	Other (specify)	Production Coordinator	Course Integrator	Programmer	Graphic Artist	Multimedia Developer	Editor	Learning Objects Specialist	Quality Assurance	Other (specify)	Evaluation Specialist	Instructional Designer	Interface Designer	Other (e.g., Pilot Subjects)	Delivery Coordinator	Systems Administrator	Server/Database Programmer	Other (specify)

Are all e-learning materials created based on the institution's stated technology requirements?

☐ Yes
☐ No
☐ Not applicable
☐ Other (specify)

Indicate timeline for project activities and responsible individuals (for example, Mrs. Smith is responsible for developing test items for lesson 1):

Activity	Project Manager	Business Developer	Consultant / Advisor	Design Coordinator	Content or Subject Matter Expert	Instructional Designer	Interface Designer	Copyright Coordinator	Evaluation Specialist	Production Coordinator	Course Integrator	Programmer	Graphic Artist	Multimedia Developer	Editor	Learning Objects Specialist	Quality Assurance	Delivery Coordinator	Systems Administrator	Server/Database Programmer	Other (specify)	Start Dare	End Date	
Test items for lesson 1								Smith														May 12	May 26	Same Test format will be used in other lessons.

Managing Content Development Process

Check the roles and responsibilities of individuals listed below during various stages of e-learning. (Note: some individuals may assume multiple roles.) Check all that apply:

Role of Individual	E-Learning Stages				
	Planning	*Design*	*Production*	*Evaluation*	*Delivery*
Director					
Project Manager					
Business Developer					
Consultant / Advisor					
Other (specify)					
Research and Design Coordinator					
Content or Subject Matter Expert					
Instructional Designer					
Interface Designer					
Copyright Coordinator					
Other (specify)					
Production Coordinator					
Course Integrator					
Programmer					
Graphic Artist					
Multimedia Developer					
Photographer/Videographer (cameraman)					
Editor					
Learning Objects Specialist					
Quality Assurance					
Pilot Subjects					
Other (specify)					
Evaluation Specialist					
Other (specify)					
Delivery Coordinator					
Systems Administrator					
Server/Database Programmer					
Other (specify					

Is there a project support site (PSS) for e-learning design, development, evaluation and delivery teams?

❑ Yes
❑ No
❑ Not applicable

If *yes*, check if the PSS has any of the following. (check all that apply):

 ❑ File upload feature to exchange documents by team members
 ❑ Project progress
 ❑ Start and end dates for each task
 ❑ The project delivery date (e.g., course is completed)
 ❑ Document updates
 ❑ Updates of new resources
 ❑ Minutes from face-to-face meetings
 ❑ Minutes from online conferencing
 ❑ Team members' email addresses
 ❑ Team members' phone numbers
 ❑ Team members' mobile phone numbers
 ❑ Team members' fax numbers
 ❑ Project due dates
 ❑ Meeting information (date, time and place)
 ❑ Graphics relevant to the project
 ❑ Audio files relevant to the project
 ❑ Video files relevant to the project
 ❑ Other (specify)

Is there a knowledge management (KM) site?

❑ Yes
❑ No
❑ Not applicable
❑ Other (specify)

List the content, contributor and copyright information for the knowledge management site:

List Contents Needed for KM	Status of Contents		Contributor Name	Require Permission?		
	Need to Create	*Already Exist*		*Yes*	*No*	*NA*

Does the institution acquire permission to use copyrighted materials for its knowledge management (KM) system from the individual copyright holders who work in the institution?
❑ Yes
❑ No
❑ Not applicable
❑ Other

Does the institution acquire permission to use copyrighted materials for its knowledge management (KM) system from copyright holders outside the institution?
❑ Yes
❑ No
❑ Not applicable
❑ Other

Does the knowledge management (KM) system have ongoing review processes to amend, delete and update its information?
❑ Yes
❑ No
❑ Not applicable
❑ Other

Managing Delivery and Maintenance

Does the course provide test make-ups for students who get disconnected from the course Website during the test?
❑ Yes
❑ No
❑ Not applicable
❑ other (please describe below)

Do students get notified when course Websites are not available, for example, down for maintenance or upgrades?
❑ Yes
❑ No
❑ Not applicable

Are the course materials updated regularly (e.g., are Web pages maintained, up to date, etc.)?
❑ Yes
❑ No
❑ Not applicable

Is the date of the revision or update being displayed prominently?
- ❑ Yes
- ❑ No
- ❑ Not applicable

Does the course inform students who is responsible for updates?
- ❑ Yes
- ❑ No
- ❑ Not applicable

Is there a link to send comments and suggestions for the Website or course?
- ❑ Yes
- ❑ No
- ❑ Not applicable

Check if students are notified about any changes in due dates or other course relevant matters (e.g., if the server hosting the course goes down) via any of the following. Check all that apply:
- ❑ E-mail
- ❑ Announcement page
- ❑ Alert boxes
- ❑ Running footer added to a page
- ❑ Phone call
- ❑ Mail
- ❑ Other (specify)
- ❑ Not applicable

Check if any of the following security measures are implemented in the course. Check all that apply:
- ❑ Login with password
- ❑ Digital signature
- ❑ Firewall
- ❑ Randomization of test questions to prevent sharing of answers
- ❑ Other (specify)

Does the course have encryption (i.e., a secure coding system) available for students to send confidential information over the Internet?
- ❑ Yes
- ❑ No
- ❑ Not applicable
- ❑ Other (specify)

Does the course have encryption (i.e., a secure coding system) available for online payment?
❑ Yes
❑ No
❑ Not applicable
❑ Other (specify)

Is this course password protected so that only enrolled students have access to this course?
❑ Yes
❑ No
❑ Not applicable

Does the course provide students with designated and secure (e.g., password protected) online spaces to store their personal notes and resources?
❑ Yes
❑ No
❑ Not applicable

Does the course have archives of previous students' discussion forum transcripts on topical issues?
❑ Yes
❑ No
❑ Not applicable

Can a hacker change contents of the course Web pages?
❑ Yes
❑ No
❑ Not applicable
❑ Not sure

Can outsiders crash the online course?
❑ Yes
❑ No
❑ Not applicable
❑ Not sure

Does the course protect students' information from outsiders (hackers)?
❑ Yes
❑ No
❑ Not applicable
❑ Other (specify)

Are unregistered individuals given access to any part of the course?
❑ Yes
❑ No
❑ Not applicable
If *yes*, list types of contents/materials that unregistered individuals can have access to:

Is there any other reliable way to submit assignments for an online class?
❑ Yes
❑ No
❑ Not applicable
If *yes*, check all that apply:
    ❑ Students can send assignments on disks
    ❑ Students can send hard copies of assignments
    ❑ Students can provide the addresses of their personal Websites where their assignments or projects are located
    ❑ Other (specify)

Does the course have a system of keeping records of student interactions? (Note: This is a privacy issue. Students' permission may be needed to use their postings).
❑ Yes
❑ No
❑ Not applicable
If *yes*, check all types of interactions:
    ❑ Between students
    ❑ Between students and instructor(s)
    ❑ N/A
    ❑ Other (specify below)

Which division of the academic institution, corporation or vendor does offer the course? Check all that apply:

Settings	Course Offered By						
	Distance Education Office	Continuing Education	Academic Department	Training Department	Human Resources Office	Individual Faculty / Trainer	Other
Academic							
Corporate							
Vendor							
Other							

Does the course have the space to store student projects and products?
☐ Yes
☐ No
☐ Not applicable
☐ Other (specify)

Does the course allow students to print out the online contents of the Web pages?
(Note: This may be useful for students who prefer reading them off-line.
However, sometimes, unnecessary blank pages are printed in addition to actual
Web pages. Course designers should minimize this problem by providing special
tips to users to avoid printing blank pages.)
☐ Yes
☐ No
☐ Not applicable

Does the course have page counters? (Note: Page counters are useful for students
to keep track of where they are in relation to the lesson. For example, 1 of 5
pages.)
☐ Yes
☐ No
☐ Not applicable

Check if any of the following supplemental materials are used in the course.
Check all that apply:
☐ Books
☐ e-books
☐ Videotape
☐ Audiotape
☐ CD-ROM
☐ Printed packet
☐ Other
☐ Not applicable

Check if the course provides a brief biography of any of the following. Check all
that apply:

Role of Individual	Yes	No	NA	Other (specify)
Instructor				
Tutor				
SME or Content Expert				
Technical Support				
Library Support				
Counselor				
Other				

Does the course provide back-up materials or alternative activities for students (i.e., what will students do?) if any of the following is either not operating properly or unavailable during a scheduled lesson period?
- ❑ Yes
- ❑ No
- ❑ Not applicable

If *yes*, check all that apply:
- ❑ Access to the courseware
- ❑ Discussion forum
- ❑ Chat room
- ❑ E-mail and mailing list
- ❑ Books
- ❑ e-books
- ❑ Online resources
- ❑ Library materials
- ❑ Study guide
- ❑ Instructor
- ❑ Tutor
- ❑ Technical support
- ❑ Other (specify)

Does the course syllabus provide any of the following options? Check all that apply:
- ❑ Course description and overview
- ❑ Course goals/objectives
- ❑ Course calendar
- ❑ Instructor's synchronous office hours
- ❑ Instructor's contact information
- ❑ Technical support staff's contact information
- ❑ Technical support staff's synchronous office hours
- ❑ Schedule of readings
- ❑ Assignments/projects information
- ❑ Assignments/projects due dates
- ❑ Attendance policy
- ❑ Late assignment policy
- ❑ Online discussion participation requirement policy
- ❑ Academic dishonesty policy
- ❑ Exams administration
- ❑ Grades
- ❑ Technology requirements
- ❑ Required textbook
- ❑ Recommended texts
- ❑ e-books
- ❑ Course relevant resources (on the Web)
- ❑ Other (specify)

Does the course indicate whether the course content is best viewed by a specific browser?
- ❑ Yes
- ❑ No
- ❑ Not applicable

Does the course indicate whether the course content is best viewed by a specific monitor display (e.g., 800, 1024, etc.)?
- ❑ Yes
- ❑ No
- ❑ Not applicable

If *yes*, please indicate the screen size:

Does the course provide a class distribution list (list containing student e-mail addresses) for students?
- ❑ Yes
- ❑ No
- ❑ Not applicable

Does the course provide a list containing students' telephone numbers to be used by other students in the course? (Note: Students permission may be needed to make their telephone numbers available to other students.)
- ❑ Yes
- ❑ No
- ❑ Not applicable

Does the course provide a list containing students' addresses? (Note: Students permission may be needed to make their addresses available to others.)
- ❑ Yes
- ❑ No
- ❑ Not applicable

Does the course provide the option for students to create their personal Web pages?
- ❑ Yes
- ❑ No
- ❑ Not applicable

Identify the ideal person for the roles and responsibilities required during the instructional stage of e-learning process. Check all that apply:

Name of the Person Ideal for the Job	Administrative							Instructional									Learner Support						
	Project Manager	Admission	Registration	Payment	Bookstore	Financial Aid		Online Course Coordinator	Instructor (or Trainer)	Instructor Assistant	Tutor	Discussion Facilitator/Moderator	Learning Objects Specialist	Copyright Coordinator	Guest Speaker (or outside Expert)		Delivery Coordinator	Systems Administrator	Server/Database Programmer	Customer Service	Technical Support Specialist	Library Services	Counseling Services

Does the course have a system of keeping track of student submissions, online quizzes, etc.?
❑ Yes
❑ No
❑ Not applicable

How often do the instructor or technical support staff check the accessibility of the course Website?
❑ Daily
❑ Weekly
❑ Monthly
❑ Other (specify)

Does the course track attendance in the discussion forum?
❑ Yes
❑ No
❑ Not applicable

Does the course have a system of reminding students about upcoming assignments?
❑ Yes
❑ No
❑ Not applicable

If *yes*, how are students reminded? Check all that apply:
- ❑ Email
- ❑ Phone
- ❑ Announcement on the course Website
- ❑ Other (specify)

Does the instructor acknowledge receipt of assignments within:
- ❑ 24 hours of initial receipt
- ❑ 48 hours of initial receipt
- ❑ 72 hours of initial receipt
- ❑ Other
- ❑ Not applicable

Does the course keep a computer log with data about learners' participation in online discussions?
- ❑ Yes
- ❑ No
- ❑ Not applicable

If *yes*, does the log data include any of the following? Check all that apply:
- ❑ Number of posts
- ❑ Time spent on each discussion topic
- ❑ Other (specify)

When does the instructor return students' assignment with feedback and grade?
- ❑ Within 7 days of initial receipt
- ❑ Within 10 days of initial receipt
- ❑ Within 14 days of initial receipt
- ❑ Other (specify)
- ❑ Not applicable

Is each student's progress monitored regularly?
- ❑ Yes
- ❑ No
- ❑ Not applicable

If *yes*, how (describe below)?

Are students contacted if their assignments are not received on time?
- ❑ Yes
- ❑ No
- ❑ Not applicable

Does the course have a private space for student interaction (for example a student "lounge" or "cafe" where there is no faculty surveillance?)
- ❑ Yes
- ❑ No
- ❑ Not applicable

Does the course have an automatic response mechanism which can send confirmation of receipt of assignments or other submissions immediately?
- ❑ Yes
- ❑ No
- ❑ Not applicable

Does this course provide a direct link to send messages for help if students are having problems?
- ❑ Yes
- ❑ No
- ❑ Not applicable

Can learners (or participants) link to outside Websites (as references) from their postings on the course discussion forum? (Note: Online articles or documents relevant to discussion topics can enhance the quality and the validity of postings.)
- ❑ Yes
- ❑ No
- ❑ Not applicable

Does the course allow students to do online editing of their already submitted (existing) documents? (Note: This may be useful for students who want to edit their already published materials for the Web-based courses.)
- ❑ Yes
- ❑ No
- ❑ Not applicable

Does the course allow students to upload their documents (or files) to the course Website?
- ❑ Yes
- ❑ No
- ❑ Not applicable

Does the course Website have an option for students to submit their assignments online?
- ❑ Yes
- ❑ No
- ❑ Not applicable

Does the course allow students to leave or broadcast messages for the entire class, cohort, group or program (bulletin board, listserv, etc.)?
- ❑ Yes
- ❑ No
- ❑ Not applicable

Does the course provide a place for groups to work on documents?
❑ Yes
❑ No
❑ Not applicable

Does the course allow students to replace an existing document by simply uploading the new document? (Note: This may be useful for students who want to replace an already published document with new changes.)
❑ Yes
❑ No
❑ Not applicable

Does the course have a mechanism to help students convert and upload students' presentation slides which are created using presentation software such as PowerPoint?
❑ Yes
❑ No
❑ Not applicable

TECHNOLOGICAL

Infrastructure Planning

Does the institution have a technology plan that clearly describes the process of acquiring, maintaining, and upgrading hardware and software required for e-learning?
- ❑ Yes
- ❑ No
- ❑ Not applicable
- ❑ Other (specify)

Check if the institution's network system has any of the following characteristics of a stable, long-lived, and widely available technology infrastructure? (check all that apply):
- ❑ Scalable
- ❑ Sustainable
- ❑ Reliable
- ❑ Consistently available
- ❑ Other (specify)

Does the course have orientation programs that provide technical training to students before starting the course?
- ❑ Yes
- ❑ No
- ❑ Not applicable
- ❑ Other (specify)

Does the institution have personnel who can assist learners in setting up their computers before starting the course?
- ❑ Yes
- ❑ No
- ❑ Not applicable

Is the course Website hosted on the course provider's own system?
- ❑ Yes
- ❑ No
- ❑ Not applicable

If *no*, check all that apply
- ❑ Hosted on a commercial system (with monthly fee)
- ❑ Hosted on an outside system (free of charge)
- ❑ Other (specify)

Does the course provide the following information about the institution's network system to learners?

❑ Bandwidth capacity
❑ Limitations of its networks
❑ Not applicable
❑ Other (specify)

Is there a "buddy system" established in the course so that learners will have at least one person who they can call to do some preliminary troubleshooting or just ask advice?

❑ Yes
❑ No
❑ Other (specify)

What happens to a pre-scheduled exam or chat when the server is down?

❑ Exam or chat is rescheduled
❑ Exam or chat is postponed until the server is up and running
❑ Exam is done offline
❑ Not applicable
❑ Not sure
❑ Other(specify)

How efficient was the course server in offering access to the course Web pages?

❑ Very efficient
❑ Efficient
❑ Fair
❑ Good
❑ Poor
❑ Not applicable
❑ Other (specify)

Does the course provide alternative off-line learning activities if the course server goes down?

❑ Yes
❑ No

Does the course provide toll-free numbers where students can dial to connect to the Internet/Web free of charge?

❑ Yes
❑ No
❑ Not applicable
❑ Other (specify)

Does the course provide a list of Internet Service Providers (ISPs) with which learners reported having encountered problems in accessing and using the course

Website? (Note: An institution cannot recommend, endorse, or promote any specific ISP best suited to the course requirement. Therefore, it cannot provide a list of Internet Service Providers best suited to the course requirements.)

❑ Yes
❑ No
❑ Not applicable
❑ Other (specify)

Does the course provide e-mail accounts to students?

❑ Yes
❑ No
❑ Not applicable

If *yes*, specify the storage space or disk quota per student:

If some students do not have enough computer expertise or skills to participate in the course, does the course offer any training sessions or direct students to appropriate resources so that they can get the necessary skills to fully participate in the various activities of the course?

❑ Yes
❑ No
❑ Not applicable
❑ Other (specify)

Is a learner's full participation in the course tied to accessing the technological components at specific times? (Note: If the course requires students to participate in synchronous activities, there will be designated times when students need to be at their course workstations. If the workstation is at home and the student is at his/her office during those times, this becomes an issue. In some circumstances, it may be cost effective for students to use PDAs, tablet PCs or other devices. However, students should check whether PDAs and other devices can use the course if it is only designed for regular PCs.)

❑ Yes
❑ No
❑ Not applicable

Are the minimum capabilities (e.g., browser, software compatibility, data transfer speeds) for an adequate Internet service provider specified in the course?

❑ Yes
❑ No
❑ Not applicable

Is there any financial aid available for students to purchase the necessary technology required for the course?

❑ Yes

❑ No

❑ Not applicable

Check if any of the following individuals have any of the following digital literacy skills. Check all that apply:

Role of Individuals	Digital Technology Skills																							
	Browser			Search Engines			File Transfer (ftp)			Scanner			Digital Camera			Creating CDs			Terms and Jargon			Other		
	Yes	No	NA	Yes	No	NA	Yes	No	NA	Yes	No	NA	Yes	No	NA	Yes	No	NA	Yes	No	NA	Yes	No	NA
Learner																								
Instructor (full-time)																								
Instructor (part-time)																								
Trainer																								
Trainer Assistant																								
Tutor																								
Technical Support																								
Help Desk																								
Librarian																								
Counselor																								
Graduate Assistant																								
Administrator																								
Other (specify)																								

Has the institution created any reusable and shareable learning objects or LOs (i.e., smallest pieces of learning contents)?

❑ Yes

❑ No

❑ Not applicable

If *yes*, check all that apply

    ❑ Individuals within the institution can use without permission (free of charge)

    ❑ Individuals within the institution can use with permission (free of charge)

    ❑ Individuals outside the institution can use without permission (free of charge)

    ❑ Individuals outside the institution can use with permission (free of charge)

    ❑ Individuals outside the institution can use (with fees)

    ❑ Other (specify)

Are learning objects created following international interoperability standards?
❏ Yes
❏ No
❏ Not applicable
If *yes*, specify the standards (e.g. SCORM)

If appropriate, are all learning objects available in the course reusable?
❏ Yes
❏ No
❏ Not applicable

Is there a search facility to search for various learning objects within the institution?
❏ Yes
❏ No
❏ Not applicable

Can learning objects available in the institution be used by its own students for their projects?
❏ Yes
❏ No
❏ Not applicable
If *yes*, check all that apply:
    ❏ Can use them without the permission of the institution
    ❏ Cannot use them without the permission of the institution
    ❏ Can use them with a fee
    ❏ Other
    ❏ Not applicable

Can learning objects available in the institution be used by outsiders?
❏ Yes
❏ No
❏ Not applicable
If *yes*, check all that apply:
    ❏ Anyone can use without the permission from the institution
    ❏ Cannot use without the permission of the institution
    ❏ Can use with a fee
    ❏ Other
    ❏ Not applicable

Is the cost of required hardware, software and the types of Internet connection (e.g., T1, DSL, cable modem, etc.) a deterrent to taking this course?
❏ Yes
❏ No
❏ Not applicable

Does the institution have special arrangements with vendors to offer students special prices for hardware and/or software?
❏ Yes
❏ No
❏ Not applicable
If *yes*, list below:

Hardware and Software	Vendor Name	Price

Are any disk quotas allocated for students in their accounts on the institution's server?
❏ Yes
❏ No
❏ Not applicable
If *yes*, can student request for increased disk quotas for special projects?
    ❏ Yes
    ❏ No
    ❏ Other (specify)

Are students given specific guidelines on how much computer expertise they need to have to participate in the course? (For example, a list of things they should know how to do on the Internet.)
❏ Yes
❏ No
❏ Not applicable

Are there time limits for how long learners can be logged on to the course?
❏ Yes
❏ No
❏ Not applicable
❏ Other (specify)

Hardware

Are the hardware requirements clearly stated in the course?
❏ Yes
❏ No

Check for all hardware requirements. If appropriate, note the specifications for each component. (Note: In the specifications section of the table, you can add as much information as possible for each component. For example, for the hard disk's *size,* specify how many gigabytes is required or recommended; for the CD-ROM drive, specify the required or recommended *speed* 24x or 32x; for RAM, specify the required or recommended *memory size,* 32, 64, 128 or 256 MB; for the monitor, specify the required or recommended *resolution* 640X480, 800X600 or 1024X768, etc.)

Hardware	Check if Required	Check if Recommended	Specifications
Computer and Peripherals			
CPU			
RAM			
ROM			
Hard disk			
Monitor			
Disk drive			
CD-ROM			
CD burner			
Sound card			
Speaker			
Microphone			
Camera			
Video card			
Modem			
DVD (Digital Versatile Disc)			
Ink-jet printer			
Laser printer			
Other (specify)			
Internet Connection			
Dial-in			
DSL (Digital Subscriber Line)			
Cable modem			
T1*			
T3*			
Ethernet			
Wireless connection			
Other (specify)			
Conferencing Tools			
Digital camera			
Video camera			

---

* T1 (DS-1): High-speed digital data channel that is a high-volume carrier of voice and/or data. Often used for compressed video teleconferencing. T-1 has 24 voice channels. T-3 (DS-3): A digital channel that communicates at a significantly faster rate than T-1. A screen reader is a computer software that speaks text on the screen. Often used by individuals who are visually impaired (http://www.learningcircuits.org/glossary.html).

Other (specify)			
Other Tools			
Cell Phone			
Pager			
PDA (Personal Digital Assistant)			
eBook reader			
Screen reader			
Other (specify)			

Does the course require learners to use any new hardware not originally listed in the technology requirement for the course?

❑ Yes
❑ No
❑ Not applicable

If *yes*, are the learners informed?

    ❑ Yes
    ❑ No
    ❑ Not applicable
    ❑ Other

Check if learners receive training in any of the following. Check all that apply:

❑ How to operate a microphone
❑ How to talk on the microphone
❑ How to do audio conferencing on a PC
❑ How to do video conferencing on a PC
❑ Other (specify)
❑ Not applicable

Does the course provide for desktop videoconferencing or any other type of real-time interaction?

❑ Yes
❑ No
❑ Other (specify)
❑ Not applicable

Does the course provide links to resources where learners can learn more about required hardware and their pricing?

❑ Yes
❑ No
❑ Other (specify)
❑ Not applicable

Does the course provide any recommendations on best place(s) to buy various *hardware* components required for the course? (Note: Any such recommendations must be done without any bias or preference. A survey of learners on such issues can be conducted and the results can be posted on the course Website. Also, reviews of hardware from magazines can be useful in this regard. Neither the instructor nor the institution should endorse or promote any particular product. However, if a hardware company is a sponsor or has a special arrangement with the institution to offer special prices for students, then it is a different issue.)

❑ Yes
❑ No
❑ Not applicable

Does the course inform students that the video clips or streaming media[1] (if any) used in the course may not run effectively with a slow modem?

❑ Yes
❑ No
❑ Not applicable

Does the course allow learners to choose any of the following connection speeds for any streaming media used in the course? (Note: With most production software, one can output for different connection speeds. However, if various connection speed options are not provided, Powell (2001) recommends that designers stream media at a low data rate so that individuals with a low connection speed can view it).

❑ 28.8 K
❑ 56K
❑ T1
❑ Not applicable

Software

Are the software requirements for the course clearly stated?

❑ Yes
❑ No
❑ Not applicable

If *yes*, indicate specific software name and check all that apply:

Software	Software Name	Required For			Recommended For			NA
		Learner	*Instructor*	*Other*	*Learner*	*Instructor*	*Other*	
Word Processor								
Email Package								
Presentation Program								
Spreadsheets								
Database								

---

[1] Streaming media (streaming audio or video): Audio or video files played as they are being downloaded over the Internet instead of users having to wait for the entire file to download first. Requires a media player program. (Source: http://www.learningcircuits.org/glossary.html#S)

Graphic Software								
eBook Reader Software								
Audio Video Editing Software								
Operating System								
Plug-ins								
Browsers								
Other (specify)								

Does the course add any new software not originally listed in the technology requirement for the course? (Note: Sometimes, instructor may add a new software after the course is started. This may not be well received by some students as it was not listed before.)
❑ Yes
❑ No
❑ Not applicable
If *yes*, are the learners informed?
   ❑ Yes
   ❑ No
   ❑ Not applicable
   ❑ Other

Are any browser "plug-ins" needed to use the pages?
❑ Yes
❑ No
❑ Not applicable
If *yes*, are they commonly used and free (such as Acrobat)?
   ❑ Yes
   ❑ No
   ❑ Not applicable

If plug-ins are necessary, is there a link to download them?
❑ Yes
❑ No
❑ Not applicable
❑ Other (specify)

Does the course provide links to resources where learners can learn more about required software and their pricing?
❑ Yes
❑ No
❑ Not applicable

Does the course provide any recommendation on the best place(s) to buy the required *software* for the course? (Note: Any such recommendations must be done without any bias or preference. A survey of learners on such issues can be conducted and the results can be posted on the course Website. Also, reviews of

software from magazines can be useful in this regard. Neither the instructor nor the institution should endorse or promote any particular product. However, if a software company is a sponsor or has special arrangement with the institution to offer special prices for students, then it is a different issue.)
❑ Yes
❑ No
❑ Not applicable

Does the course provide links to resources where all necessary software can be downloaded or purchased?
❑ Yes
❑ No
❑ Not applicable

If there are applets or other software to download, does the course specify operating system, memory, CPU and bandwidth requirements?
❑ Yes
❑ No
❑ Not applicable

Check if the course provides any of the following interaction or communication mechanisms for students. (check all that apply):
❑ Chat
❑ E-mail
❑ MUD (Multi-User Dungeon or Dimension)[2]
❑ MOO (Mud, Object Oriented)
❑ Discussion Forum
❑ Newsgroup
❑ Whiteboard
❑ Other (describe below)

Is the course developed using any of the following software? (check all that apply):
❑ LMS
❑ LCMS
❑ Authoring software
❑ Other (specify)
If yes, check if the software is in compliance with any of the following standards. (check all that apply):
    ❑ Institute for Electrical and Electronic Engineers (IEEE)
    ❑ Instructional Management Systems (IMS)
    ❑ AICC (Aviation Industry CBT Committee)
    ❑ SCORM (Sharable Courseware Object Reference Model)
    ❑ All of the above

---

[2] http://www.pit.ktu.lt/HP/coper/kiev.new/cit/gloslz.htm#MUD

❑ Other (describe below)

Are there any criteria used to select LMS, LCMS or the authoring tool? (Note: An article entitled "Selecting a Learning Management System" is available at: http://www.e-learninghub.com/articles/learning_management_system.html. Also, a resources site entitled "Selecting and Using Tools" is available at: http://www.e-learningcentre.co.uk/eclipse/Resources/default-selecting.htm which provides information about LMS, LCMS and authoring tools.).
❑ Yes
❑ No
❑ Not applicable
❑ Other (specify)

If appropriate, check the functionality of the LMS used at the institution. (Note: adopted from http://www.bctechnology.com/statics/pstacey-oct2601.html. Check all that apply:
❑ Schedules and registers learners into online and offline courses
❑ Keeps learner profile data
❑ Launches e-learning courses
❑ Tracks learner progress through courses
❑ Manages classroom based learning
❑ Provides learning administrators with the ability to manage learning resources including labs and classrooms (resource management)
❑ Supports learner collaboration
❑ Automates use of competency maps to define career development and performance paths (skills gap analysis)
❑ Creation of test questions and administration of test
❑ Performance reporting learning results
❑ Interconnectivity with Virtual Classroom (VC), LCMS and enterprise applications
❑ Other (specify)

If appropriate, check the functionality of the LCMS used at the institution. (Note: adopted from *http://www.bctechnology.com/statics/pstacey-oct2601.html*. Check all that apply:
❑ Content migration and management
❑ Content creation tools
❑ Workflow tools to manage content development process
❑ Learning object repository
❑ Organizing reusable content
❑ Content reuse and adaptive individualized learning paths based on learning objects
❑ Asynchronous collaborative learning including discussion groups
❑ Testing and certification
❑ Reporting of results
❑ Delivering content in multiple formats (online, print, PDA, CD-ROM, etc.)
❑ Providing content navigational controls (look and feel)

❑ Interconnectivity with Virtual Classroom, LMS and enterprise applications

Does the LMS, LCMS or other software used in creating the course work with newer versions of a variety of browsers?
❑ Yes
❑ No
❑ Not applicable
❑ Other (specify)

Does the institution use enterprise application software?
❑ Yes
❑ No
❑ Not applicable
❑ Other (specify)
If *yes*, can LMS, LCMS or authoring tool used for e-learning be integrated with the institution's enterprise software?
  ❑ Yes
  ❑ No
  ❑ Not applicable
  ❑ Other (specify

PEDAGOGICAL

Content Analysis

Is the content of the course accurate?
- ❑ Yes
- ❑ No
- ❑ Not applicable
- ❑ Other (specify)

Given the course goals, is the content complete?
- ❑ Yes
- ❑ No
- ❑ Not applicable

If *yes*, list the topics within a content area that would be suitable for e-learning, face-to-face instruction and/or other.

Topics	Content Suitability Analysis		
	E-Learning	*Face-to-Face*	*Other*
1.			
2.			
3.			
4.			
5.			
5.			
6.			
7.			
8.			

List stable and dynamic contents for each lesson. (Note: Content that does not need to be updated can be categorized as *static*. For example, historical events, grammar rules, etc. Content that has the potential to change over time can be considered *dynamic*. For example, laws, policies, etc.).

Lesson Name	E-Learning Content Stability Analysis	
	List *Stable* Contents	List *Dynamic* Contents

How often is the dynamic course content updated?
- ❏ Weekly
- ❏ Monthly
- ❏ Quarterly
- ❏ Yearly
- ❏ As needed
- ❏ Not applicable
- ❏ Other (specify)

Check all that applies for content types in each lesson or unit of the course.

Content Types	Lesson or Unit									
	1	2	3	4	5	6	7	8	9	10
Facts										
Concepts										
Processes										
Principles										
Procedures										
Other (specify)										

Check all that apply for the types of reading assignments recommended for online and offline activities of the course:

Types of Reading Assignments	Online Activity	Offline Activity	Other (specify)
Required textbook(s)			
Readings from books other than textbook(s)			
Readings from printed-based journal/magazine			
Readings from online magazine and journal			
Readings from e-books			
Case study			
Readings located at the course Website			
Readings located in non-course Website			
Readings from CD-ROM			
Reference materials			
Other (specify)			

Does the course require students to do any offline activities (e.g., physical and hands-on activities such as viewing particular TV programs, visiting learning centers, library, etc.)?
- ❏ Yes
- ❏ No
- ❏ Not applicable

If *yes*, please specify:

Does a course's description in the syllabus communicate the importance and relevance of its content?
- ❑ Yes
- ❑ No
- ❑ Not applicable
- ❑ Other (specify)

Is the description of the course in the syllabus the same as the one approved by the curriculum committee? (Note: E-learning designers should always refer to the approved documents. If any changes are made in the syllabus, learners should be notified.)
- ❑ Yes
- ❑ No
- ❑ Not applicable
- ❑ Other (specify)

Does the course content use any textual and multimedia materials from outside sources?
- ❑ Yes
- ❑ No
- ❑ Not applicable
- ❑ Other (specify)

If *yes*, check all that apply:
- ❑ Textual and multimedia materials used in the course represent a variety of viewpoints
- ❑ Accurate information about where the materials came from is provided
- ❑ Other (specify)

Audience Analysis

Does the institution have any of the following demographic information available about learners? (check all that apply):

Demographic Information	Yes	No	NA	Other
Age range				
Gender				
Educational level				
Grade-point average (GPA)				
Standardized test scores (e.g., SAT, GRE)				
Socioeconomic background				
Racial/ethnic background				
Physical disabilities				
Learning disabilities				

Does the institution have any of the following knowledge and skills information available about learners? (Note: If the institution does not have information about learners' knowledge and skills, e-learning designers should proactively do surveys to gather such information.)

Knowledge and Skills Information	Yes	No	NA	Other
Writing skills				
Reading skills				
Mathematical skills				
Communication skills				
Keyboarding skills				
Word processing skills				
Internet navigation skills				
Previous experience with e-learning				
Ability to work independently				
Ability to work with culturally diverse learners				
Familiarity with various instructional methods				
Familiarity with different delivery systems				
Other (specify)				

If any of the following information is available about learners, check all that apply for their knowledge and skills level:

Knowledge and Skills Information	Level				
	Excellent	Good	Fair	Good	NA
Writing skills					
Reading skills					
Mathematical skills					
Communication skills					
Keyboarding skills					
Word processing skills					
Internet navigation skills					
Previous experience with e-learning					
Ability to work independently					
Ability to work with culturally diverse learners					
Familiarity with various instructional methods					
Familiarity with different delivery systems					
Other (specify)					

Does the institution have any of the following learning preferences information available about learners? (Note: If the institution does not have such information, e-learning designers should proactively do surveys to find out what learners prefer.)

Learning Preferences	Yes	No	NA	Other
Lecture				
Presentation				
Exhibits				
Demonstration				

Drill and Practice				
Tutorials				
Games				
Storytelling				
Simulations				
Role-playing				
Discussion				
Interaction				
Modeling				
Facilitation				
Collaboration				
Debate				
Field Trips				
Apprenticeship				
Case Studies				
Other (specify)				

Does the institution have information about learners' preferred learning styles (e.g., visual/nonverbal, visual/verbal, auditory and kinesthetic)? (Note: If the institution does not have information about learners' preferred learning styles, e-learning designers should proactively do surveys to gather such information. The l2earner diversity section discusses learning styles.)

❏ Yes
❏ No
❏ Not applicable
❏ Other (specify)

If *yes*, write a summary of the target population's preferred learning styles.

Does the institution have any of the following attitudinal and motivational information available about learners? (check all that apply):

Attitudinal and Motivational Information	Yes	No	NA	Other
Motivation level				
Interests				
Anxiety level				
Attitude toward learning				
Attitude toward instructional content of the course				
Learners' expectations concerning the course content				
Learners' expectations concerning instructional delivery				

Do learners have some background knowledge or skills that are needed to start the e-learning course?

❏ Yes
❏ No
❏ Not applicable
❏ Other (specify)

Do learners have previous experience with e-learning?
- ❑ Yes
- ❑ No
- ❑ Not applicable
- ❑ Other (specify)

What kinds of expectations do learners have concerning instructional delivery?

_____

_____

_____

_____

Goal Analysis

Does the course survey students before instruction begins in order to identify what they expect to learn or gain from the course?
- ❑ Yes
- ❑ No
- ❑ Not applicable
- ❑ Other (specify)

Are any of the following important aspects of an instructional goal considered in establishing each goal in the course?
- ❑ The learners
- ❑ The learning context
- ❑ The tools and technologies available to learners
- ❑ Other (specify)

How relevant is the instructional goal of the course to the learners?
- ❑ Highly relevant
- ❑ Moderately relevant
- ❑ Not relevant at all
- ❑ Not applicable
- ❑ Other (specify)

Are the course goal(s) approved by appropriate officials within the institution?
- ❑ Yes
- ❑ No
- ❑ Not applicable
- ❑ Other (specify)

OURO COLLÉGE LIBRARY

Are there adequate resources (e.g., personnel, time, etc.) to develop e-learning lessons for the proposed course goal(s)?
❑ Yes
❑ No
❑ Not applicable
❑ Other (specify)

Check the appropriate course structure format for e-learning?
❑ Course → Unit → Lesson
❑ Other
❑ Not applicable

Outline the course structure below:

Course Name	Unit Name	Lesson Name
(For example) 101. Instructional design (ID)	(For example) 101.1 Introduction to ID	(For example) 101.1.1 Components of Systems approach Model
101.	101.1	101.1.1
		101.1.2
	101.2	101.2.1
		101.2.2
	101.3	101.3.1
		101.3.2
	101.4	101.4.1
		101.4.2

Length of learning units (check appropriate option):
❑ Less than 10 minutes
❑ 10 – 20 minutes
❑ 21 – 30 minutes
❑ 31 – 40 minutes
❑ 41 – 50 minutes
❑ Self-paced (depends on individual's progress)
❑ Instructor led
❑ Other
❑ NA

JURO COLLEGE LIBRARY

Does the course provide the following? (check all that apply):

Goals and Objectives	Yes	No	NA	Other
Course Goals				
Course Objectives				
Unit/Chapter Goals				
Unit/Chapter Objectives				
Lesson Goals				
Lesson Objectives				
Other (specify)				

Are clear learning outcomes specified in the course?
❑ Yes
❑ No
❑ Not applicable

Does the course provide clear descriptions of what capabilities learners will possess, what they should know or be able to do after completing the course?
❑ Yes
❑ No
❑ Not applicable

Are all required lesson objectives identified (that must be learned to achieve the lesson goal)?
❑ Yes
❑ No
❑ Not applicable

If appropriate, check all that apply for lesson objectives. Are they
❑ Measurable
❑ Achievable
❑ Not applicable
❑ Other (specify)

Does the course inform learners what they must do to achieve the objectives?
❑ Yes
❑ No
❑ Not applicable

Are course assignments, reports and discussions flexible enough to accommodate students' own learning goals?
❑ Yes
❑ No
❑ Not applicable

Do the course goals and objectives include the skills covered in similar courses taught in other institutions?
- ❑ Yes
- ❑ No
- ❑ Not applicable

Does the course review the prerequisite skills necessary for learning the skills of the course?
- ❑ Yes
- ❑ No
- ❑ None needed
- ❑ Not applicable

Media Analysis

Check if the course can use a variety of delivery media for its various lessons/units. Check all that apply:

Lesson	Delivery Media					
	Internet	CD-ROM	DVD	Print-Based Materials	Face-to-Face Class	Other
1.						
2.						
3.						
4.						
5.						
6.						

Which presentation modes does the course use? (check all that apply):
- ❑ Text
- ❑ Graphics
- ❑ Audio
- ❑ Video
- ❑ Animation
- ❑ Not applicable
- ❑ Other (specify below)

How effective was the mixture of multimedia attributes in creating a rich environment for active learning?
- ❑ Very effective
- ❑ Moderately effective
- ❑ Not effective
- ❑ Not applicable
- ❑ Other

Does the course exploit the flexibility of the hypertext/hypermedia (e.g., hyperlinks) environment of the Web?
❏ Yes
❏ No
❏ Not applicable

Is the course content appropriately matched to the method of delivery?
❏ Yes
❏ No
❏ Not applicable
If no, describe below:

Design Approach

What type of content does the course deal with?
❏ Well-structured
❏ Ill-structured
❏ Combination of both (check the appropriate option from below)
    ❏ About equal percent of well-structured or ill-structured contents
    ❏ More well-structured than ill-structured contents
    ❏ More ill-structured than well-structured contents
    ❏ Other (specify)

Check the appropriate pedagogical philosophy for domain types: (check all apply)

Domain Type	Pedagogical Philosophy			
	Instructivist	Constructivist	Eclectic or Combination	Other (specify)
Well-structured				
Ill-structured				

Check the instructor's role (check all that apply):
❏ Domain expert
❏ Facilitator
❏ Coach
❏ Mentor
❏ Eclectic
❏ Not sure
❏ Other (specify)

Does the course allow for the instructor to serve as facilitator?
❏ Yes
❏ No

❑ Not applicable
If *yes*, how/where does facilitation occur? Can it occur in environments using any or all of the following Internet tools? (check all that apply):

    ❑ E-mail
    ❑ Mailing list
    ❑ Online discussion forum
    ❑ Chat
    ❑ Audio conference
    ❑ Video conference
    ❑ Virtual classroom
    ❑ Other (specify)

What is the learner's role?
❑ Passive: A recipient of information
❑ Active: Active participant in creating knowledge from within
❑ Combination
❑ Not Applicable
❑ Not sure
❑ Other (specify below)

Does the course provide metacognition support by including annotations on online documents or resources?
❑ Yes
❑ No
❑ Not applicable
If *yes*, please describe how problems are presented and solved:

Please check the relevant control of learning activities used in the course.
❑ Student-centered (students control their own learning activities)
❑ Program-centered (students follows a structured environment)
❑ Combination of both
❑ Not sure

Is the course designed to support students to become independent distance learners?
❑ Yes
❑ No
❑ Not applicable
If *yes*, please specify how:

If the course allows students to have some control over the material to be learned, check all that apply:
❑ Students choose topics for course projects
❑ Students write up discussion questions

❑ Students select the path to navigate through instructions
❑ Students negotiate learning goals
❑ Select working group
❑ Students negotiate evaluation criteria
❑ Students have flexible due dates
❑ Other (specify)

If the course material is to some degree controlled by the program, check all that apply:
❑ Program determines the course's topics
❑ Program imposes the course's structure
❑ Program dictates the path through the instruction
❑ Program prescribes the learning goals
❑ Instructor forms teams for group projects
❑ Instructor leads discussions
❑ Instructor schedules exam dates
❑ Other (specify)

Organization

Does the course provide clear directions of what learners should do at every stage of the course?
❑ Yes
❑ No
❑ Not applicable

Does the course provide a sense of continuity for the learners (i.e., each unit of the lesson builds on the previous unit where appropriate)?
❑ Yes
❑ No
❑ Not applicable

Are the course materials organized in a manner appropriate to the apparent philosophical approach (instructivist, constructivist, or combination of both, etc.)?
❑ Yes, course material are organized following an instructivist instructional design approach
❑ Yes, course material are organized following a constructivist instructional design approach
❑ Yes, course material are organized following a combination of both instructivist and constructivist instructional design approach
❑ No
❑ Not applicable
❑ Other (specify)

Is there a clear and apparent sequence or structure to the information?
❑ Yes
❑ No
❑ Not applicable

Whenever appropriate, is the material grouped ("chunked") effectively?
❑ Yes
❑ No
❑ Not applicable

Does the course provide summaries of key points of the instruction?
❑ Yes
❑ No
❑ Not applicable

Learning Strategies[3]

Does the course have *online presentation(s)*?
❑ Yes
❑ No
❑ Not applicable
If *yes*, how effective were *online presentations* (check all that apply)?

Role of Individual	Performance Level				
	Excellent	*Good*	*Fair*	*Poor*	*NA*
Instructor					
Guest Speaker					
Students					
Other (specify)					

Are any of the following multimedia components, Internet tools, and
supplementary materials used in *presentations*? (check all that apply):

I. Multimedia components
    ❑ Text
    ❑ Graphics
    ❑ Audio
    ❑ Animation
    ❑ Video

---

[3] Please note that the author maintains a resource Website entitled "E-Learning Methods and Strategies" at **http://BooksToRead.com/elearning/strategies.htm** which provides links to relevant Websites dealing with various methods and strategies included in this section.

❑ Other (specify)
II. Internet tools
    ❑ E-mail
    ❑ Mailing lists
    ❑ Newsgroups
    ❑ Bulletin boards
    ❑ Chat
    ❑ Messaging
    ❑ Multi-user dialogues
    ❑ Computer conferencing
    ❑ Links to outside Websites
    ❑ Other (specify)
III. Supplementary materials
    ❑ CD-ROM
    ❑ DVD
    ❑ Videotape
    ❑ eBook
    ❑ Print (books/articles)
    ❑ Other (specify)
IV. Other (specify below)

Evaluate the *instructional* (e.g., learning related) and *technical* (e.g., bandwidth, file size, production quality, connectivity, etc.) effectiveness of the multimedia components, Internet tools, and supplementary materials in *presentations*.(check all that apply):

	Instructional Effectiveness					Technical Effectiveness				
	Excellent	*Good*	*Fair*	*Poor*	*NA*	*Excellent*	*Good*	*Fair*	*Poor*	*NA*
Multimedia components										
Text										
Graphics										
Photographs										
Audio										
Narration										
Animation										
Video										
Other (specify)										
Internet tools										
E-mail										
Mailing lists										
Newsgroups										
Bulletin boards										
Chat										
Messaging										
Multi-user dialogues										
Computer conferencing										
Outside Website links										
Other (specify)										

Supplementary materials									
CD-ROM									
DVD									
Videotape									
eBook									
Print (books/articles)									
Other (specify)									

Does the course have virtual *exhibits*?
❑ Yes
❑ No
❑ Not applicable
If *yes*, how effective were virtual *exhibits* used in the course?
   ❑ Very effective
   ❑ Moderately effective
   ❑ Not effective
   ❑ Other (specify)

Are all visuals and objects used in the digital *exhibits* organized with a clear description?
❑ Yes
❑ No
❑ Not applicable
❑ Other (specify)

Are any of the following multimedia components, Internet tools, and supplementary materials used in *exhibits*? (check all that apply):
I. Multimedia components
   ❑ Text
   ❑ Graphics
   ❑ Audio
   ❑ Animation
   ❑ Video
   ❑ Other (specify)
II. Internet tools
   ❑ E-mail
   ❑ Mailing lists
   ❑ Newsgroups
   ❑ Bulletin boards
   ❑ Chat
   ❑ Messaging
   ❑ Multi-User dialogues
   ❑ Computer conferencing
   ❑ Links to outside Websites
   ❑ Other (specify)
III. Supplementary materials

❑ CD-ROM
❑ DVD
❑ Videotape
❑ eBook
❑ Print (books, articles, etc.)
❑ Other (specify)

IV. Other (specify below)

Evaluate the *instructional* (e.g., learning related) and *technical* (e.g., bandwidth, file size, production quality, connectivity, etc.) effectiveness of the multimedia components, Internet tools, and supplementary materials in the instructional *exhibits*. (check all that apply):

	Instructional Effectiveness					Technical Effectiveness				
	Excellent	*Good*	*Fair*	*Poor*	*NA*	*Excellent*	*Good*	*Fair*	*Poor*	*NA*
Multimedia components										
Text										
Graphics										
Photographs										
Audio										
Narration										
Animation										
Video										
Other (specify)										
Internet tools										
E-mail										
Mailing lists										
Newsgroups										
Bulletin boards										
Chat										
Messaging										
Multi-user dialogues										
Computer conferencing										
Outside Website links										
Other (specify)										
Supplementary materials										
CD-ROM										
DVD										
Videotape										
eBook										
Print (books/articles)										
Other (specify)										

Does the course provide online *demonstration* sessions?
❑ Yes
❑ No
❑ Not applicable

If *yes*, how effective were the *demonstration* sessions?

❑ Very effective
❑ Moderately effective
❑ Not effective
❑ Other (specify)

Are any of the following multimedia components, Internet tools, and supplementary materials used in the instructional *demonstrations*? (check all that apply):

I. Multimedia components
    ❑ Text
    ❑ Graphics
    ❑ Audio
    ❑ Animation
    ❑ Video
    ❑ Other (specify)

II. Internet tools
    ❑ E-mail
    ❑ Mailing lists
    ❑ Newsgroups
    ❑ Bulletin boards
    ❑ Chat
    ❑ Messaging
    ❑ Multi-user dialogues (MUDs)
    ❑ Computer conferencing
    ❑ Links to outside Websites
    ❑ Other (specify)

III. Supplementary materials
    ❑ CD-ROM
    ❑ DVD
    ❑ Videotape
    ❑ eBook
    ❑ Print (books, articles, etc.)
    ❑ Other (specify)

IV. Other (specify below)

Evaluate the *instructional* (e.g., learning related) and *technical* (e.g., bandwidth, file size, production quality, connectivity, etc.) effectiveness of the multimedia components, Internet tools, and supplementary materials in the *demonstration* sessions. (check all that apply):

	Instructional Effectiveness					Technical Effectiveness				
	Excellent	*Good*	*Fair*	*Poor*	*NA*	*Excellent*	*Good*	*Fair*	*Poor*	*NA*
Multimedia components										
Text										
Graphics										
Photographs										

Audio						
Narration						
Animation						
Video						
Other (specify)						
Internet tools						
E-mail						
Mailing lists						
Newsgroups						
Bulletin boards						
Chat						
Messaging						
Multi-user dialogues						
Computer Conferencing						
Outside Website links						
Other (specify)						
Supplementary materials						
CD-ROM						
DVD						
Videotape						
eBook						
Print (books/articles)						
Other (specify)						

Does the course provide online *drill and practice* sessions?
❑ Yes
❑ No
❑ Not applicable
If *yes*, how effective were the *drill and practice* sessions?
    ❑ Very effective
    ❑ Moderately effective
    ❑ Not effective
    ❑ Other (specify)

Are any of the following Multimedia components, Internet tools, supplementary materials used in *drill and practice*? (check all that apply):
I. Multimedia components
    ❑ Text
    ❑ Graphics
    ❑ Audio
    ❑ Animation
    ❑ Video
    ❑ Other (specify)
II. Internet tools
    ❑ E-mail
    ❑ Mailing lists
    ❑ Newsgroups

   ❑ Bulletin boards
   ❑ Chat
   ❑ Messaging
   ❑ Multi-user dialogues (MUDs)
   ❑ Computer conferencing
   ❑ Links to outside Websites
   ❑ Other (specify)

III. Supplementary materials
   ❑ CD-ROM
   ❑ DVD
   ❑ Videotape
   ❑ eBook
   ❑ Print (books, articles, etc.)
   ❑ Other (specify)

IV. Other (specify below)

Evaluate the *instructional* (e.g., learning related) and *technical* (e.g., bandwidth, file size, production quality, connectivity, etc.) effectiveness of the multimedia components, Internet tools, and supplementary materials in the *drill and practice* sessions. (check all that apply):

	Instructional Effectiveness					Technical Effectiveness				
	Excellent	*Good*	*Fair*	*Poor*	*NA*	*Excellent*	*Good*	*Fair*	*Poor*	*NA*
Multimedia components										
Text										
Graphics										
Photographs										
Audio										
Narration										
Animation										
Video										
Other (specify)										
Internet tools										
E-mail										
Mailing lists										
Newsgroups										
Bulletin boards										
Chat										
Messaging										
Multi-user dialogues										
Computer conferencing										
Outside Website links										
Other (specify)										
Supplementary materials										
CD-ROM										
DVD										
Videotape										
eBook										

Print (books/articles)											
Other (specify)											

Does the course provide online *tutorial* sessions?
- ❏ Yes
- ❏ No
- ❏ Not applicable

If *yes*, how effective were the *tutorial* sessions?
- ❏ Very effective
- ❏ Moderately effective
- ❏ Not effective
- ❏ Other (specify)

Are any of the following multimedia components, Internet tools, and supplementary materials used in the *tutorials*? (check all that apply):

I. Multimedia components
- ❏ Text
- ❏ Graphics
- ❏ Audio
- ❏ Animation
- ❏ Video
- ❏ Other (specify)

II. Internet tools
- ❏ E-mail
- ❏ Mailing lists
- ❏ Newsgroups
- ❏ Bulletin boards
- ❏ Chat
- ❏ Messaging
- ❏ Multi-user dialogues (MUDs)
- ❏ Computer conferencing
- ❏ Links to outside Websites
- ❏ Other (specify)

III. Supplementary materials
- ❏ CD-ROM
- ❏ DVD
- ❏ Videotape
- ❏ eBook
- ❏ Print (books/articles)
- ❏ Other (specify)

IV. Other (specify below)

Evaluate the *instructional* (e.g., learning related) and *technical* (e.g., bandwidth, file size, production quality, connectivity, etc.) effectiveness of the multimedia components, Internet tools, and supplementary materials in the *tutorials*. (check all that apply):

	Instructional Effectiveness					Technical Effectiveness				
	Excellent	*Good*	*Fair*	*Poor*	*NA*	*Excellent*	*Good*	*Fair*	*Poor*	*NA*
Multimedia components										
Text										
Graphics										
Photographs										
Audio										
Narration										
Animation										
Video										
Other (specify)										
Internet tools										
E-mail										
Mailing lists										
Newsgroups										
Bulletin boards										
Chat										
Messaging										
Multi-user dialogues										
Computer conferencing										
Outside Website links										
Other (specify)										
Supplementary materials										
CD-ROM										
DVD										
Videotape										
eBook										
Print (books/articles)										
Other (specify)										

Does the course use any *story-telling* technique?
❑ Yes
❑ No
❑ Not applicable
If *yes*, how effective were the *storytelling* techniques?
    ❑ Very effective
    ❑ Moderately effective
    ❑ Not effective
    ❑ Other (specify)

Are any of the following multimedia components, Internet tools, and supplementary materials used in the *storytelling*? (check all that apply):
I. Multimedia components
    ❑ Text
    ❑ Graphics
    ❑ Audio
    ❑ Animation
    ❑ Video

☐ Other (specify)
II. Internet tools
    ☐ E-mail
    ☐ Mailing lists
    ☐ Newsgroups
    ☐ Bulletin boards
    ☐ Chat
    ☐ Messaging
    ☐ Multi-user dialogues (MUDs)
    ☐ Computer conferencing
    ☐ Links to outside Websites
    ☐ Other (specify)
III. Supplementary materials
    ☐ CD-ROM
    ☐ DVD
    ☐ Videotape
    ☐ eBook
    ☐ Print (books/articles)
    ☐ Other (specify)
IV. Other (specify below)

Evaluate the *instructional* (e.g., learning related) and *technical* (e.g., bandwidth, file size, production quality, connectivity, etc.) effectiveness of the multimedia components, Internet tools, and supplementary materials in the instructional *storytelling*. (check all that apply):

	Instructional Effectiveness					Technical Effectiveness				
	Excellent	*Good*	*Fair*	*Poor*	*NA*	*Excellent*	*Good*	*Fair*	*Poor*	*NA*
Multimedia components										
Text										
Graphics										
Photographs										
Audio										
Narration										
Animation										
Video										
Other (specify)										
Internet tools										
E-mail										
Mailing lists										
Newsgroups										
Bulletin boards										
Chat										
Messaging										
Multi-user dialogues										
Computer conferencing										
Outside Website links										
Other (specify)										

Supplementary materials										
CD-ROM										
DVD										
Videotape										
eBook										
Print (books/articles)										
Other (specify)										

Does the course use online *games*?
- ❏ Yes
- ❏ No
- ❏ Not applicable

If *yes*, how effective were the *games* sessions?
- ❏ Very effective
- ❏ Moderately effective
- ❏ Not effective
- ❏ Other (specify)

Are any of the following multimedia components, Internet tools, and supplementary materials used in the *games*? (check all that apply):

I. Multimedia components
- ❏ Text
- ❏ Graphics
- ❏ Audio
- ❏ Animation
- ❏ Video
- ❏ Other (specify)

II. Internet tools
- ❏ E-mail
- ❏ Mailing lists
- ❏ Newsgroups
- ❏ Bulletin boards
- ❏ Chat
- ❏ Messaging
- ❏ Multi-user dialogues (MUDs)
- ❏ Computer conferencing
- ❏ Links to outside Websites
- ❏ Other (specify)

III. Supplementary materials
- ❏ CD-ROM
- ❏ DVD
- ❏ Videotape
- ❏ eBook
- ❏ Print (books/articles)
- ❏ Other (specify)

IV. Other (specify below)

Evaluate the *instructional* (e.g., learning related) and *technical* (e.g., bandwidth, file size, production quality, connectivity, etc.) effectiveness of the multimedia components, Internet tools, and supplementary materials in the *game* sessions. (check all that apply):

	Instructional Effectiveness					Technical Effectiveness				
	Excellent	*Good*	*Fair*	*Poor*	*NA*	*Excellent*	*Good*	*Fair*	*Poor*	*NA*
Multimedia components										
Text										
Graphics										
Photographs										
Audio										
Narration										
Animation										
Video										
Other (specify)										
Internet tools										
E-mail										
Mailing lists										
Newsgroups										
Bulletin boards										
Chat										
Messaging										
Multi-user dialogues										
Computer conferencing										
Outside Website links										
Other (specify)										
Supplementary materials										
CD-ROM										
DVD										
Videotape										
eBook										
Print (books/articles)										
Other (specify)										

Does the course use online *simulation*?
❑ Yes
❑ No
❑ Not applicable
If *yes*, how effective were the *simulation* sessions?
  ❑ Very effective
  ❑ Moderately effective
  ❑ Not effective
  ❑ Other (specify)

Are any of the following multimedia components, Internet tools, and supplementary materials used in the *simulations*? (check all that apply):

I. Multimedia components
- ❑ Text
- ❑ Graphics
- ❑ Audio
- ❑ Animation
- ❑ Video
- ❑ Other (specify)

II. Internet tools
- ❑ E-mail
- ❑ Mailing lists
- ❑ Newsgroups
- ❑ Bulletin boards
- ❑ Chat
- ❑ Messaging
- ❑ Multi-user dialogues (MUDs)
- ❑ Computer conferencing
- ❑ Links to outside Websites
- ❑ Other (specify)

III. Supplementary materials
- ❑ CD-ROM
- ❑ DVD
- ❑ Videotape
- ❑ eBook
- ❑ Print (books/articles)
- ❑ Other (specify)

IV. Other (specify below)

Evaluate the *instructional* (e.g., learning related) and *technical* (e.g., bandwidth, file size, production quality, connectivity, etc.) effectiveness of the multimedia components, Internet tools, and supplementary materials in *simulations*. (check all that apply):

	Instructional Effectiveness					Technical Effectiveness				
	Excellent	*Good*	*Fair*	*Poor*	*NA*	*Excellent*	*Good*	*Fair*	*Poor*	*NA*
Multimedia components										
Text										
Graphics										
Photographs										
Audio										
Narration										
Animation										
Video										
Other (specify)										
Internet tools										
E-mail										
Mailing lists										
Newsgroups										

Bulletin boards											
Chat											
Messaging											
Multi-user dialogues											
Computer conferencing											
Outside Website links											
Other (specify)											
Supplementary materials											
CD-ROM											
DVD											
Videotape											
eBook											
Print (books/articles)											
Other (specify)											

Does the course provide *role-playing* sessions?
❑ Yes
❑ No
❑ Not applicable
If yes, were simulated *role portrayals* facilitated through:
  ❑ Multi-User Dialogue (MUD) environments, in which instructors create
     virtual space with a central theme, characters, and artifacts.
  ❑ Problem-based case studies
  ❑ Other (specify below)

How effective were the *role-playing* sessions?
❑ Very effective
❑ Moderately effective
❑ Not effective
❑ Not applicable
❑ Other (specify below)

Are any of the following multimedia components, Internet tools, and
supplementary materials used in the *role-playing*? (check all that apply):
I. Multimedia components
  ❑ Text
  ❑ Graphics
  ❑ Audio
  ❑ Animation
  ❑ Video
  ❑ Other (specify)
II. Internet tools
  ❑ E-mail
  ❑ Mailing lists
  ❑ Newsgroups
  ❑ Bulletin boards

       ❑ Chat
       ❑ Messaging
       ❑ Multi-user dialogues (MUDs)
       ❑ Computer conferencing
       ❑ Links to outside Websites
       ❑ Other (specify)

III. Supplementary materials
       ❑ CD-ROM
       ❑ DVD
       ❑ Videotape
       ❑ eBook
       ❑ Print (books/articles)
       ❑ Other (specify)

IV. Other (specify below)

Evaluate the *instructional* (e.g., learning related) and *technical* (e.g., bandwidth, file size, production quality, connectivity, etc.) effectiveness of the multimedia components, Internet tools, and supplementary materials in the *role-playing*. (check all that apply):

	Instructional Effectiveness					Technical Effectiveness				
	Excellent	*Good*	*Fair*	*Poor*	*NA*	*Excellent*	*Good*	*Fair*	*Poor*	*NA*
Multimedia components										
Text										
Graphics										
Photographs										
Audio										
Narration										
Animation										
Video										
Other (specify)										
Internet tools										
E-mail										
Mailing lists										
Newsgroups										
Bulletin boards										
Chat										
Messaging										
Multi-user dialogues										
Computer conferencing										
Outside Website links										
Other (specify)										
Supplementary materials										
CD-ROM										
DVD										
Videotape										
eBook										
Print (books/articles)										
Other (specify)										

Does the course provide online *asynchronous discussion* sessions?
- ❑ Yes
- ❑ No
- ❑ Not applicable

If *yes*, how effective were the online *asynchronous discussion* sessions?
- ❑ Very effective
- ❑ Moderately effective
- ❑ Not effective
- ❑ Other (specify)

Does the course provide *online synchronous discussion* sessions?
- ❑ Yes
- ❑ No
- ❑ Not applicable

If *yes*, how effective were the *online synchronous discussion* sessions?
- ❑ Very effective
- ❑ Moderately effective
- ❑ Not effective
- ❑ Other (specify)

Are any of the following multimedia components, Internet tools, and supplementary materials used in the *discussions*? (check all that apply):

I. Multimedia components
- ❑ Text
- ❑ Graphics
- ❑ Audio
- ❑ Animation
- ❑ Video
- ❑ Other (specify)

II. Internet tools
- ❑ E-mail
- ❑ Mailing lists
- ❑ Newsgroups
- ❑ Bulletin boards
- ❑ Chat
- ❑ Messaging
- ❑ Multi-user dialogues (MUDs)
- ❑ Computer conferencing
- ❑ Links to outside Websites
- ❑ Other (specify)

III. Supplementary materials
- ❑ CD-ROM
- ❑ DVD
- ❑ Videotape
- ❑ eBook

❑ Print (books/articles)
❑ Other (specify)
IV. Other (specify below)

Evaluate the *instructional* (e.g., learning related) and *technical* (e.g., bandwidth, file size, production quality, connectivity, etc.) effectiveness of the multimedia components, Internet tools, and supplementary materials in the *discussion* sessions. (check all that apply):

	Instructional Effectiveness					Technical Effectiveness				
	Excellent	*Good*	*Fair*	*Poor*	*NA*	*Excellent*	*Good*	*Fair*	*Poor*	*NA*
Multimedia components										
Text										
Graphics										
Photographs										
Audio										
Narration										
Animation										
Video										
Other (specify)										
Internet tools										
E-mail										
Mailing lists										
Newsgroups										
Bulletin boards										
Chat										
Messaging										
Multi-user dialogues										
Computer conferencing										
Outside Website links										
Other (specify)										
Supplementary materials										
CD-ROM										
DVD										
Videotape										
eBook										
Print (books/articles)										
Other (specify)										

Does the course instructor/facilitator post ground rules for the discussion forum?
❑ Yes
❑ No
❑ Not applicable

Does the course instructor/facilitator intervene when conflicts get personal in the discussion forum?
❑ Yes
❑ No
❑ Not applicable

Does the instructor or facilitator start the synchronous discussion session on time? (Note: if the facilitator is late, the learners may log off. In face-to-face classes learners may wait few a minutes or look for the instructor around the building, but online that may not happen. It should be noted that synchronous sessions sometimes may not start on time due to technical difficulties.)
❑ Yes
❑ No
❑ Not applicable

Are asynchronous discussion topics used in the course relevant to the goals and objectives of the course?
❑ Yes
❑ No
❑ Not applicable

Are synchronous discussion topics used in the course relevant to the goals and objectives of the course?
❑ Yes
❑ No
❑ Not applicable

Does the course require students to participate in scheduled online discussions?
❑ Yes
❑ No
❑ Not applicable

Does the course give students an opportunity to serve as online discussion leaders?
❑ Yes
❑ No
❑ Not applicable
❑ Other (specify)

Does the instructor/facilitator send private e-mails to those who are not participating in ongoing discussions?
❑ Yes
❑ No
❑ Not applicable

Does the instructor/facilitator send private e-mails to those whose messages appear to flame others on the class list?
❑ Yes
❑ No
❑ Not applicable

How does the instructor/facilitator communicate with individuals whose messages appear to flame others in the class list? (check all that apply):
❑ Private e-mail
❑ Telephone
❑ Online chat
❑ Online discussion
❑ Letter
❑ Other (specify)

Does the instructor/facilitator send private e-mails to those whose writings may be improved?
❑ Yes
❑ No
❑ Not applicable

Does the instructor/facilitator post encouraging messages on the list for students whose posts were thoughtful and relevant to the topic?
❑ Yes
❑ No
❑ Not applicable

Are learners advised to use a word processor in preparing their postings for discussion forums? (Note: I encourage my students to use the word processor for preparing their discussion form responses and save them on their hard drives. This way they can check spelling errors and grammar before posting it on the discussion forum. In the case of server failures, they can always retrieve their postings from their hard drives. However, some might argue that worrying about errors and typos can greatly inhibit students and waste their time.)
❑ Yes
❑ No
❑ Not applicable
❑ Other (specify)

Do students receive guidance on writing and online behavior on discussion forums?
❑ Yes
❑ No
❑ Not applicable
If yes, check all that apply:
    ❑ How to write effective postings on discussion forums
    ❑ How to compose a response
    ❑ How to behave (netiquette) on a discussion forum
    ❑ Other

Are students encouraged to read and comment on each others' postings on online discussions?

❑ Yes

❑ No

❑ Not applicable

Does the instructor respond to students' postings on the discussion forum?

❑ Yes

❑ No

❑ Not applicable

If *yes*, check all that apply:

    ❑ Instructor responds to each student's posting.

    ❑ Instructor only responds to those postings where students ask for the instructor's attention.

    ❑ Instructor only responds to those postings to which a response seems appropriate, in the instructor's judgment.

    ❑ Instructor does not respond to students' postings on the discussion forums.

Does the instructor post online discussion topics on set dates (or at a scheduled time)?

❑ Yes

❑ No

❑ Not applicable

Are students required to submit discussion topics for class discussion?

❑ Yes

❑ No

❑ Recommended but not required

❑ Not applicable

❑ Other

Are students expected to assume a leadership role in moderating specific discussion topics at some time during the course?

❑ Yes

❑ No

❑ Not applicable

Does the instructor summarize and analyze the discussion at the end of each discussion topic?

❑ Yes

❑ No

❑ Not applicable

Does the instructor intervene appropriately when online discussions go in the wrong direction?

❑ Yes
❑ No
❑ Not applicable
❑ Other (specify)

Does the instructor/moderator encourage students to keep their posts brief and
relevant to the discussion topic?
❑ Yes
❑ No
❑ Not applicable

Is the course discussion forum easy to use?
❑ Yes
❑ No
❑ Not applicable

Do students receive training in the use of the discussion forum?
❑ Yes
❑ No
❑ Not applicable

Does the course require or recommend that students subscribe to course relevant
discussion forums?
❑ Yes
❑ No
❑ Not applicable
If *yes*, check all that apply:

Subscription	Required	Recommended
Class listserv		
Professional organizations' discussion lists		
Other (specify)		

Does the course instructor (or facilitator) signal the end of the on-going discussion
by summarizing the discussion?
❑ Yes
❑ No
❑ Not applicable

Is the instructor (or facilitator) sensitive about potential information overload
from the large flow of text generated from a discussion forum?
❑ Yes
❑ No
❑ Not applicable
If *yes*, any preventive measures considered (please specify)

Does the course have a system of archiving synchronous discussions? (Note: This type of archive will be useful for students who cannot participate in live chats or who missed the live online discussion sessions. There is software that allows both voice and chat to be archived: http://www.horizonlive.com)
❑ Yes
❑ No
❑ Not applicable

Do the synchronous online discussion sessions provide for breaks (e.g., lunch breaks and periodical breaks)?
❑ Yes
❑ No
❑ Not applicable
If *yes*, are they time zone sensitive?

How many participants are allowed to chat at the same time in synchronous environments? (It can be difficult to create effective live discussion sessions with too many learners actively participating.)
❑ Less than 10
❑ 10 – 20
❑ 21 – 30
❑ 31 – 40
❑ 41 – 50
❑ Not applicable
❑ Other

Are learners expected to do any asynchronous homework assignments before participating in a synchronous online discussion session?
❑ Yes
❑ No
❑ Not applicable

Are learners expected to have any specific materials in front of them during synchronous online discussion sessions?
❑ Yes
❑ No
❑ Not applicable
If *yes*, check all that apply:
    ❑ Reading materials
    ❑ Calculator
    ❑ PowerPoint slides
    ❑ Notebook
    ❑ Not applicable
    ❑ Other (specify)

Does the course incorporate *interaction* as an instructional method?
- ❏ Yes
- ❏ No
- ❏ Not applicable

If *yes*, how effective were the *interactive* sessions?
- ❏ Very effective
- ❏ Moderately effective
- ❏ Not effective
- ❏ Other (specify)

Are any of the following multimedia components, Internet tools, and supplementary materials used in the *interactive sessions*? (check all that apply):

I. Multimedia components
- ❏ Text
- ❏ Graphics
- ❏ Audio
- ❏ Animation
- ❏ Video
- ❏ Other (specify)

II. Internet tools
- ❏ E-mail
- ❏ Mailing lists
- ❏ Newsgroups
- ❏ Bulletin boards
- ❏ Chat
- ❏ Messaging
- ❏ Multi-user dialogues (MUDs)
- ❏ Computer conferencing
- ❏ Links to outside Websites
- ❏ Other (specify)

III. Supplementary materials
- ❏ CD-ROM
- ❏ DVD
- ❏ Videotape
- ❏ eBook
- ❏ Print (books/articles)
- ❏ Other (specify)

IV. Other (specify below)

Evaluate the *instructional* (e.g., learning related) and *technical* (e.g., bandwidth, file size, production quality, connectivity, etc.) effectiveness of the multimedia components, Internet tools, and supplementary materials in the *discussion* sessions. (check all that apply):

	Instructional Effectiveness					Technical Effectiveness				
	Excellent	*Good*	*Fair*	*Poor*	*NA*	*Excellent*	*Good*	*Fair*	*Poor*	*NA*
Multimedia components										
Text										
Graphics										
Photographs										
Audio										
Narration										
Animation										
Video										
Other (specify)										
Internet tools										
E-mail										
Mailing lists										
Newsgroups										
Bulletin boards										
Chat										
Messaging										
Multi-user dialogues										
Computer conferencing										
Outside Website links										
Other (specify)										
Supplementary materials										
CD-ROM										
DVD										
Videotape										
eBook										
Print (books/articles)										
Other (specify)										

Does the course encourage students to make comments about each other's assignments in the online discussion forum?
❏ Yes
❏ No
❏ Not applicable

Does the course encourage students to set up their own peer study groups?
❏ Yes
❏ No
❏ Not applicable

Is learner-learner interaction encouraged in the course?
❏ Yes
❏ No

❑ Not applicable

Does the course support interactions through the use of any of the following (check all that apply)?
❑ Peer evaluation
❑ Help sessions
❑ Collaborative projects
❑ Online study groups
❑ Not applicable
❑ Other (specify)

Is the course interactive?
❑ Yes
❑ No
❑ Not applicable
If *yes*, check all that apply:
        ❑ Among students?
        ❑ Between students and teacher(s)?
        ❑ With online resources?

How effective were the interactions?
❑ Very effective
❑ Moderately effective
❑ Not effective
❑ Not applicable

Does the course incorporate *modeling* as an instructional method?
❑ Yes
❑ No
❑ Not applicable
If *yes*, *modeling* is facilitated by:
        ❑ modeling behavior in electronic communication environments
        ❑ providing samples of relevant coursework
        ❑ providing guidance for interactions in simulated environments such as MUDs (Multi-User Dialogues)
        ❑ Other (specify below)

How effective were the *modeling* sessions?
❑ Very effective
❑ Moderately effective
❑ Not effective
❑ Not applicable
❑ Other (specify)

Are any of the following multimedia components, Internet tools, and supplementary materials used in the *modeling*? (check all that apply):

I. Multimedia components
- ❑ Text
- ❑ Graphics
- ❑ Audio
- ❑ Animation
- ❑ Video
- ❑ Other (specify)

II. Internet tools
- ❑ E-mail
- ❑ Mailing lists
- ❑ Newsgroups
- ❑ Bulletin boards
- ❑ Chat
- ❑ Messaging
- ❑ Multi-user dialogues (MUDs)
- ❑ Computer conferencing
- ❑ Links to outside Websites
- ❑ Other (specify)

III. Supplementary materials
- ❑ CD-ROM
- ❑ DVD
- ❑ eBook
- ❑ Print (books/articles)
- ❑ Other (specify)

IV. Other (specify below)

Evaluate the *instructional* (e.g., learning related) and *technical* (e.g., bandwidth, file size, production quality, connectivity, etc.) effectiveness of the multimedia components, Internet tools, and supplementary materials in the *modeling* sessions. (check all that apply):

	Instructional Effectiveness					Technical Effectiveness				
	Excellent	*Good*	*Fair*	*Poor*	*NA*	*Excellent*	*Good*	*Fair*	*Poor*	*NA*
Multimedia components										
Text										
Graphics										
Photographs										
Audio										
Narration										
Animation										
Video										
Other (specify)										
Internet tools										
E-mail										

Mailing lists											
Newsgroups											
Bulletin boards											
Chat											
Messaging											
Multi-user dialogues											
Computer conferencing											
Outside Website links											
Other (specify)											
Supplementary materials											
CD-ROM											
DVD											
eBook											
Print (books/articles)											
Other (specify)											

Does the course use the instructional method of *facilitation* by providing guidance to students, directing discussion, suggesting possible resources, fielding questions, etc?

❑ Yes

❑ No

❑ Not applicable

If *yes*, please check all that apply:

Through asynchronous communication tools such as:

❑ E-mail

❑ Discussion forums

❑ Newsgroups

❑ Bulletin boards

❑ Web-based threaded discussions

❑ Not applicable

❑ Other (specify below)

Through synchronous communication tools such as:

❑ Chat

❑ Multi-user dialogues (MUDs)

❑ Audio conferencing

❑ Video conferencing

❑ Not applicable

❑ Other (specify below)

How effective were the *facilitation* sessions?

❑ Very effective

❑ Moderately effective

❑ Not effective

❑ Not applicable

❑ Other (specify)

Are any of the following multimedia components, Internet tools, and
supplementary materials used in the *facilitation*? (check all that apply):
I. Multimedia components
- ❑ Text
- ❑ Graphics
- ❑ Audio
- ❑ Animation
- ❑ Video
- ❑ Other (specify)

II. Internet tools
- ❑ E-mail
- ❑ Mailing lists
- ❑ Newsgroups
- ❑ Bulletin boards
- ❑ Chat
- ❑ Messaging
- ❑ Multi-user dialogues (MUDs)
- ❑ Computer conferencing
- ❑ Links to outside Websites
- ❑ Other (specify)

III. Supplementary materials
- ❑ CD-ROM
- ❑ DVD
- ❑ Videotape
- ❑ eBook
- ❑ Print (books/articles)
- ❑ Other (specify)

IV. Other (specify below)

Evaluate the *instructional* (e.g., learning related) and *technical* (e.g., bandwidth,
file size, production quality, connectivity, etc.) effectiveness of the multimedia
components, Internet tools, and supplementary materials used in the service of
course *facilitation*. (check all that apply):

	Instructional Effectiveness					Technical Effectiveness				
	Excellent	*Good*	*Fair*	*Poor*	*NA*	*Excellent*	*Good*	*Fair*	*Poor*	*NA*
Multimedia components										
Text										
Graphics										
Photographs										
Audio										
Narration										
Animation										
Video										
Other (specify)										
Internet tools										
E-mail										

Mailing lists												
Newsgroups												
Bulletin boards												
Chat												
Messaging												
Multi-user dialogues												
Computer conferencing												
Outside Website links												
Other (specify)												
Supplementary materials												
CD-ROM												
DVD												
Videotape												
eBook												
Print (books/articles)												
Other (specify)												

Does the facilitator help learners focus on relevant issues in the discussion forum?
❑ Yes
❑ No
❑ Not applicable

Does the facilitator encourage learners to ask questions?
❑ Yes
❑ No
❑ Not applicable

Does the facilitator arouse interest and curiosity among learners?
❑ Yes
❑ No
❑ Not applicable

Does the facilitator encourage learners to elaborate their responses on issues discussed in the discussion forum?
❑ Yes
❑ No
❑ Not applicable

Does the facilitator encourage learners to reflect and self-evaluate?
❑ Yes
❑ No
❑ Not applicable

Does the facilitator provide a list of experts with whom learners can communicate via e-mail to solicit expert opinions on issues related to their course projects?
❑ Yes
❑ No

❑ Not applicable
❑ Other (specify)

Does the facilitator provide customized responses for individual inquiries?
❑ Yes
❑ No
❑ Not applicable

Does the course provide a list of Frequently Asked Questions (FAQs) to handle questions that are asked over and over again?
❑ Yes
❑ No
❑ Not applicable

Does the course direct learners to explore external sites where they can analyze and compare materials? (Note: Such exploratory activities allow learners to make the materials relevant to their own needs and increase their motivation level.)
❑ Yes
❑ No
❑ Not applicable

Indicate the facilitator's level of involvement in facilitating online learning activities throughout the course?
❑ High-level involvement
❑ Mid-level involvement
❑ Low-level involvement
❑ Not applicable

Does the course promote *inside collaboration* by providing a supportive environment for asking questions, clarifying directions, suggesting or contributing resources, and class members working on joint projects?
❑ Yes
❑ No
❑ Not applicable
If *yes*, please check all that apply:
    Through asynchronous communication tools such as:
    ❑ E-mail
    ❑ Discussion forums
    ❑ Newsgroups
    ❑ Bulletin boards
    ❑ Web-based threaded discussions
    ❑ Collaborative work tools that allow for shared screens
    ❑ Not applicable
    ❑ Other (specify below)
    Through synchronous communication tools such as:

- ☐ Chat room
- ☐ Multi-user dialogues (MUDs)
- ☐ Computer conferencing
- ☐ Other (specify below)

How effective were the *inside collaboration* techniques?
- ☐ Very effective
- ☐ Moderately effective
- ☐ Not effective
- ☐ Not applicable
- ☐ Other (specify)

Does the course promote *outside collaboration* by involving external personnel and resources (speakers, guest lecturers, web sites, etc.) to participate in course activities?
- ☐ Yes
- ☐ No
- ☐ Not applicable

If *yes*, please check all that apply:

    Through asynchronous communication tools such as:
- ☐ E-mail
- ☐ Discussion forum
- ☐ Newsgroups
- ☐ Bulletin boards
- ☐ Other (specify below)

    Through synchronous communication tools such as:
- ☐ Chat
- ☐ Multi-user dialogues (MUDs)
- ☐ Computer conferencing
- ☐ Other (specify below)

Does the course have guest speakers? (Note: The course instructor or facilitator should ask learners to prepare their questions in advance and limit the number of questions so that the guest is not overwhelmed with questions.)
- ☐ Yes
- ☐ No
- ☐ Not applicable

If *yes*, please check all that apply:
- ☐ Information is provided for the number of times the guest speaker(s) will be available for synchronous discussion
- ☐ Information is provided for the period that the guest speaker(s) will be available for synchronous discussion
- ☐ Information about the guest speakers' contribution is clearly indicated
- ☐ Other (specify)

How effective were the outside collaboration techniques?

❑ Very effective
❑ Moderately effective
❑ Not effective
❑ Not applicable

Are any of the following multimedia components, Internet tools, and
supplementary materials used in the *collaborative* sessions? (check all that apply):
I. Multimedia components
    ❑ Text
    ❑ Graphics
    ❑ Audio
    ❑ Animation
    ❑ Video
    ❑ Other (specify)
II. Internet tools
    ❑ E-mail
    ❑ Mailing lists
    ❑ Newsgroups
    ❑ Bulletin boards
    ❑ Chat
    ❑ Messaging
    ❑ Multi-user dialogues (MUDs)
    ❑ Computer conferencing
    ❑ Links to outside Websites
    ❑ Other (specify)
III. Supplementary materials
    ❑ CD-ROM
    ❑ DVD
    ❑ Videotape
    ❑ eBook
    ❑ Print (books/articles)
    ❑ Other (specify)
IV. Other (specify below)

Evaluate the *instructional* (e.g., learning related) and *technical* (e.g., bandwidth,
file size, production quality, connectivity, etc.) effectiveness of the multimedia
components, Internet tools, and supplementary materials in *collaborative*
sessions. (check all that apply):

	Instructional Effectiveness					Technical Effectiveness				
	Excellent	*Good*	*Fair*	*Poor*	*NA*	*Excellent*	*Good*	*Fair*	*Poor*	*NA*
Multimedia components										
Text										
Graphics										
Photographs										

Audio											
Narration											
Animation											
Video											
Other (specify)											
Internet tools											
E-mail											
Mailing lists											
Newsgroups											
Bulletin boards											
Chat											
Messaging											
Multi-user dialogues											
Computer conferencing											
Outside Website links											
Other (specify)											
Supplementary materials											
CD-ROM											
DVD											
Videotape											
eBook											
Print (books/articles)											
Other (specify)											

Does the course use *debates* as instructional activities?

❑ Yes

❑ No

❑ Not applicable

If *yes*, how effective were the online *debate* sessions?

    ❑ Very effective

    ❑ Moderately effective

    ❑ Not effective

    ❑ Other (specify)

Are any of the following multimedia components, Internet tools, and supplementary materials used in the *debates*? (check all that apply):

I. Multimedia components

    ❑ Text

    ❑ Graphics

    ❑ Audio

    ❑ Animation

    ❑ Video

    ❑ Other (specify)

II. Internet tools

    ❑ E-mail

    ❑ Mailing lists

    ❑ Newsgroups

    ❑ Bulletin boards

☐ Chat
☐ Messaging
☐ Multi-user dialogues (MUDs)
☐ Computer conferencing
☐ Links to outside Websites
☐ Other (specify)

III. Supplementary materials

☐ CD-ROM
☐ DVD
☐ Videotape
☐ eBook
☐ Print (books/articles)
☐ Other (specify)

IV. Other (specify below)

Evaluate the *instructional* (e.g., learning related) and *technical* (e.g., bandwidth, file size, production quality, connectivity, etc.) effectiveness of the multimedia components, Internet tools, and supplementary materials in the *debate* sessions. (check all that apply):

	Instructional Effectiveness					Technical Effectiveness				
	Excellent	*Good*	*Fair*	*Poor*	*NA*	*Excellent*	*Good*	*Fair*	*Poor*	*NA*
Multimedia components										
Text										
Graphics										
Photographs										
Audio										
Narration										
Animation										
Video										
Other (specify)										
Internet tools										
E-mail										
Mailing lists										
Newsgroups										
Bulletin boards										
Chat										
Messaging										
Multi-user dialogues										
Computer conferencing										
Outside Website links										
Other (specify)										
Supplementary materials										
CD-ROM										
DVD										
Videotape										
eBook										
Print (books/articles)										
Other (specify)										

Do learners receive any guidelines in any of the following critical elements of debates? Check all that apply?
❑ How to engage in an open, honest exchange of ideas
❑ How to engage in group interaction
❑ How to think critically
❑ How to express personal views effectively
❑ How to be tolerant
❑ How to resolve conflicts among debate participants
❑ Other (specify)

Does the course use virtual *field trips* as an instructional method?
❑ Yes
❑ No
❑ Not applicable
If *yes*, how effective were the online *field trips*?
     ❑ Very effective
     ❑ Moderately effective
     ❑ Not effective
     ❑ Other (specify)

Does the course provide students with a travel agenda and timetable for their online field trip?
❑ Yes
❑ No
❑ Not applicable

Are any of the following multimedia components, Internet tools, and supplementary materials used in the *field trips*? (check all that apply):
I. Multimedia components
     ❑ Text
     ❑ Graphics
     ❑ Audio
     ❑ Animation
     ❑ Video
     ❑ Other (specify)
II. Internet tools
     ❑ E-mail
     ❑ Mailing lists
     ❑ Newsgroups
     ❑ Bulletin boards
     ❑ Chat
     ❑ Messaging
     ❑ Multi-user dialogues (MUDs)

      ❑ Computer conferencing
      ❑ Links to outside Websites
      ❑ Other (specify)
III. Supplementary materials
      ❑ CD-ROM
      ❑ DVD
      ❑ Videotape
      ❑ eBook
      ❑ Print (books/articles)
      ❑ Other (specify)
IV. Other (specify below)

Evaluate the *instructional* (e.g., learning related) and *technical* (e.g., bandwidth, file size, production quality, connectivity, etc.) effectiveness of the multimedia components, Internet tools, and supplementary materials in the *field trip* sessions. (check all that apply):

	Instructional Effectiveness					Technical Effectiveness				
	Excellent	*Good*	*Fair*	*Poor*	*NA*	*Excellent*	*Good*	*Fair*	*Poor*	*NA*
Multimedia components										
Text										
Graphics										
Photographs										
Audio										
Narration										
Animation										
Video										
Other (specify)										
Internet tools										
E-mail										
Mailing lists										
Newsgroups										
Bulletin boards										
Chat										
Messaging										
Multi-user dialogues										
Computer conferencing										
Outside Website links										
Other (specify)										
Supplementary materials										
CD-ROM										
DVD										
Videotape										
eBook										
Print (books/articles)										
Other (specify)										

Does the course provide students with specific guidelines for what they should accomplish through their field trip experience?

❑ Yes
❑ No
❑ Not applicable

Does the course require students to submit reports about their field trip?
❑ Yes
❑ No
❑ Not applicable

Are students required to discuss their field trip experience on the discussion forum?
❑ Yes
❑ No
❑ Not applicable

Does the course use *apprenticeship* as an instructional method (i.e., guidance by an outside expert for a particular learning task)?
❑ Yes
❑ No
❑ Not applicable
If *yes*, please check all that apply:
    Through asynchronous communication tools such as:
    ❑ E-mail
    ❑ Discussion forums
    ❑ Newsgroups
    ❑ Bulletin boards
    ❑ Web-based threaded discussions
    ❑ Not applicable
    ❑ Other (specify below)
    Through synchronous communication tools such as:
    ❑ Chat
    ❑ Multi-user dialogues (MUDs)
    ❑ Computer conferencing
    ❑ Other (specify below)

How effective were the *apprenticeship* sessions?
❑ Very effective
❑ Moderately effective
❑ Not effective
❑ Not applicable
❑ Other (specify)

Are any of the following multimedia components, Internet tools, and supplementary materials used in the *apprenticeship* activities? (check all that apply):

I. Multimedia components
- ❑ Text
- ❑ Graphics
- ❑ Audio
- ❑ Animation
- ❑ Video
- ❑ Other (specify)

II. Internet tools
- ❑ E-mail
- ❑ Mailing lists
- ❑ Newsgroups
- ❑ Bulletin boards
- ❑ Chat
- ❑ Messaging
- ❑ Multi-user dialogues (MUDs)
- ❑ Computer conferencing
- ❑ Links to outside Websites
- ❑ Other (specify)

III. Supplementary materials
- ❑ CD-ROM
- ❑ DVD
- ❑ Videotape
- ❑ eBook
- ❑ Print (books/articles)
- ❑ Other (specify)

IV. Other (specify below)

Evaluate the *instructional* (e.g., learning related) and *technical* (e.g., bandwidth, file size, production quality, connectivity, etc.) effectiveness of the multimedia components, Internet tools, and supplementary materials used to create the *apprenticeship* sessions. (check all that apply):

	Instructional Effectiveness					Technical Effectiveness				
	Excellent	*Good*	*Fair*	*Poor*	*NA*	*Excellent*	*Good*	*Fair*	*Poor*	*NA*
Multimedia components										
Text										
Graphics										
Photographs										
Audio										
Narration										
Animation										
Video										
Other (specify)										
Internet tools										
E-mail										
Mailing lists										
Newsgroups										

Bulletin boards										
Chat										
Messaging										
Multi-user dialogues										
Computer conferencing										
Outside Website links										
Other (specify)										
Supplementary materials										
CD-ROM										
DVD										
Videotape										
eBook										
Print (books/articles)										
Other (specify)										

Does the course use *case studies*?
❑ Yes
❑ No
❑ Not applicable
If *yes*, how effective were the *case studies*?
    ❑ Very effective
    ❑ Moderately effective
    ❑ Not effective
    ❑ Other (specify)

Are any of the following multimedia components, Internet tools, and supplementary materials used in the *case studies*? (check all that apply):
I. Multimedia components
    ❑ Text
    ❑ Graphics
    ❑ Audio
    ❑ Animation
    ❑ Video
    ❑ Other (specify)
II. Internet tools
    ❑ E-mail
    ❑ Mailing lists
    ❑ Newsgroups
    ❑ Bulletin boards
    ❑ Chat
    ❑ Messaging
    ❑ Multi-user dialogues (MUDs)
    ❑ Computer conferencing
    ❑ Links to outside Websites
    ❑ Other (specify)
III. Supplementary materials

□ CD-ROM
□ DVD
□ Videotape
□ eBook
□ Print (books/articles)
□ Other (specify)
IV. Other (specify below)

Evaluate the *instructional* (e.g., learning related) and *technical* (e.g., bandwidth, file size, production quality, connectivity, etc.) effectiveness of the multimedia components, Internet tools, and supplementary materials in the *case study* sessions. (check all that apply):

	Instructional Effectiveness					Technical Effectiveness				
	Excellent	*Good*	*Fair*	*Poor*	*NA*	*Excellent*	*Good*	*Fair*	*Poor*	*NA*
Multimedia components										
Text										
Graphics										
Photographs										
Audio										
Narration										
Animation										
Video										
Other (specify)										
Internet tools										
E-mail										
Mailing lists										
Newsgroups										
Bulletin boards										
Chat										
Messaging										
Multi-user dialogues										
Computer conferencing										
Outside Website links										
Other (specify)										
Supplementary materials										
CD-ROM										
DVD										
Videotape										
eBook										
Print (books/articles)										
Other (specify)										

Does the course provide activities through which learners can generate understandings of course content? (Note: *Generative learning* can be supported by many different learning strategies.)
□ Yes
□ No
□ Not applicable

If *yes*, for a course or unit, check the *generative strategies* used (check all that apply):

- ❏ Demonstrate comprehension of the facts, concepts, etc.
- ❏ Make predictions
- ❏ Paraphrase
- ❏ Summarize
- ❏ Elaborate
- ❏ Make inferences
- ❏ Devise applications (uses)
- ❏ Create metaphors or analogies
- ❏ Think of examples
- ❏ Diagram or visualize the structure of the new content
- ❏ Other (specify)

Does the course present the learner with authentic problem-solving activities in which the learner must make decisions and experience consequences?

- ❏ Yes
- ❏ No
- ❏ Not applicable

If *yes*, please describe how problems are presented and solved:

How effective were the *generative learning* methods?

- ❏ Very effective
- ❏ Moderately effective
- ❏ Not effective
- ❏ Not applicable
- ❏ Other (specify)

Are any of the following multimedia components, Internet tools, and supplementary materials used in the *generative learning*? (check all that apply):

I. Multimedia components

- ❏ Text
- ❏ Graphics
- ❏ Audio
- ❏ Animation
- ❏ Video
- ❏ Other (specify)

II. Internet tools

- ❏ E-mail
- ❏ Mailing lists
- ❏ Newsgroups
- ❏ Bulletin boards
- ❏ Chat
- ❏ Messaging
- ❏ Multi-user dialogues (MUDs)

    ❑ Computer conferencing
    ❑ Links to outside Websites
    ❑ Other (specify)

III. Supplementary materials
    ❑ CD-ROM
    ❑ DVD
    ❑ Videotape
    ❑ eBook
    ❑ Print (books/articles)
    ❑ Other (specify)

IV. Other (specify below)

Evaluate the *instructional* (e.g., learning related) and *technical* (e.g., bandwidth, file size, production quality, connectivity, etc.) effectiveness of the multimedia components, Internet tools, and supplementary materials in any activities that involve *generative learning* sessions. (check all that apply):

	Instructional Effectiveness					Technical Effectiveness				
	Excellent	*Good*	*Fair*	*Poor*	*NA*	*Excellent*	*Good*	*Fair*	*Poor*	*NA*
Multimedia components										
Text										
Graphics										
Photographs										
Audio										
Narration										
Animation										
Video										
Other (specify)										
Internet tools										
E-mail										
Mailing lists										
Newsgroups										
Bulletin boards										
Chat										
Messaging										
Multi-user dialogues										
Computer conferencing										
Outside Website links										
Other (specify)										
Supplementary materials										
CD-ROM										
DVD										
Videotape										
eBook										
Print (books/articles)										
Other (specify)										

Does the course stimulate recall of prior knowledge?

❑ Yes
❑ No
❑ Not applicable

Does the course incorporate *motivation* as an instructional method?
❑ Yes
❑ No
❑ Not applicable
If *yes*, how effective were the *motivation* sessions?
     ❑ Very effective
     ❑ Moderately effective
     ❑ Not effective
     ❑ Other (specify)

Are any of the following multimedia components, Internet tools, and supplementary materials used to *motivate* students? (check all that apply):
I. Multimedia components
     ❑ Text
     ❑ Graphics
     ❑ Audio
     ❑ Animation
     ❑ Video
     ❑ Other (specify)
II. Internet tools
     ❑ E-mail
     ❑ Mailing lists
     ❑ Newsgroups
     ❑ Bulletin boards
     ❑ Chat
     ❑ Messaging
     ❑ Multi-user dialogues (MUDs)
     ❑ Computer conferencing
     ❑ Links to outside Websites
     ❑ Other (specify)
III. Supplementary materials
     ❑ CD-ROM
     ❑ DVD
     ❑ Videotape
     ❑ eBook
     ❑ Print (books/articles)
     ❑ Other (specify)
IV. Other (specify below)

Evaluate the *instructional* (e.g., learning related) and *technical* (e.g., bandwidth, file size, production quality, connectivity, etc.) effectiveness of the multimedia components, Internet tools, and supplementary materials used in *motivating* students. (check all that apply):

	Instructional Effectiveness					Technical Effectiveness				
	Excellent	*Good*	*Fair*	*Poor*	*NA*	*Excellent*	*Good*	*Fair*	*Poor*	*NA*
Multimedia components										
Text										
Graphics										
Photographs										
Audio										
Narration										
Animation										
Video										
Other (specify)										
Internet tools										
E-mail										
Mailing lists										
Newsgroups										
Bulletin boards										
Chat										
Messaging										
Multi-user dialogues										
Computer conferencing										
Outside Website links										
Other (specify)										
Supplementary materials										
CD-ROM										
DVD										
Videotape										
eBook										
Print (books/articles)										
Other (specify)										

Does the course address concern for learner dissonance or anxiety? (Note: Learners' anxiety can be caused by the conflict between their beginner role, their lack of experience with Internet learning technologies, and their view of traditional learning systems, as indicated by Aggarwal, 2000. It is always good to discuss learner dissonance issues during orientation or the introductory session of the course.)
❑ Yes
❑ No
❑ Not applicable
❑ Other (specify)

Does the course provide for motivational factors such as fantasy and challenge, where appropriate?
❑ Yes
❑ No

❑ Not applicable

Does the course consider the situational and topical interest factors of cognitive motivation?
❑ Yes
❑ No
❑ Not applicable

Does the course provide ways to help students who are unmotivated about e-learning?
❑ Yes
❑ No
❑ Not applicable

At the beginning, does the course set an appropriate tone/climate in order for students to feel comfortable in sharing their ideas and personal information?
❑ Yes
❑ No
❑ Not applicable

Do students receive ongoing feedback on their performance in the various learning activities?
❑ Yes
❑ No
❑ Not applicable

Does the course encourage students to actively participate and contribute in online learning activities?
❑ Yes
❑ No
❑ Not applicable
❑ Other (specify)

Does the course use real world examples for students to make connections between course material and their lives?
❑ Yes
❑ No
❑ Not applicable

Does the course provide students with choice (such as options or alternatives and a sense of control over the learning environment)?
❑ Yes
❑ No
❑ Not applicable
❑ Other (specify)

Does the course provide students with a variety of learning activities to keep them interested and attentive?
- ❏ Yes
- ❏ No
- ❏ Not applicable
- ❏ Other (specify)

Does the course use motivational factors such as surprise, novelty, and intrigue to keep students curious about online learning activities?
- ❏ Yes
- ❏ No
- ❏ Not applicable
- ❏ Other (specify)

Does the course encourage students to exchange ideas and provide feedback on each other's work?
- ❏ Yes
- ❏ No
- ❏ Not applicable
- ❏ Other (specify)

Does the course provide examples and non-examples of new concepts and principles for the learners to make comparisons?
- ❏ Yes
- ❏ No
- ❏ Not applicable

Identify appropriate methods for various lessons or units of the course. Check all that apply:

Strategy	Lesson Name	Content Description
Presentation		
Exhibits		
Demonstration		
Drill and Practice		
Tutorials		
Storytelling		
Games		
Simulations		
Role-playing		
Discussion		
Interaction		
Modeling		
Facilitation		
Collaboration		
Debate		

Field Trips		
Apprenticeship		
Case Studies		
Generative learning		
Motivation		
Other (specify)		

ETHICAL

Social and Political Influence

Does the institution have to get approval from any external entities (that can serve as political barriers) to implement its e-learning?
❑ Yes
❑ No
❑ Not applicable
If *yes*, please list the entities:

Does the course designer need internal approval from any authorities within the institution for certain e-learning content and activities?
❑ Yes
❑ No
❑ Not applicable
If *yes*, please list e-learning content types, e-learning activities and the approving authorities:

Is there a social/political preference for any particular instructional method? (Note: for example, the apprenticeship model is preferred by Norwegian political tradition.)
❑ Yes
❑ No
❑ Not applicable
If *yes*, please list the e-learning strategies most preferred:

Cultural Diversity

To improve cross-cultural verbal communication and avoid misunderstanding, does the course make an effort to reduce or avoid the use of jargon, idioms, humor, acronyms, and ambiguous words, terms and content? (Note: We should avoid using jokes or comments that can be misinterpreted and misunderstood by some.)
❑ Yes
❑ No
❑ Not applicable
If *yes*, does the course have or link to resource site(s) where interpretations of cross-cultural jargon and idioms are available?
   ❑ Yes
   ❑ No
   ❑ Not applicable

To improve visual communication, is the course sensitive to the use of navigational icons or images? (Note: For example, Reeves & Reeves in 1997 noted that a pointing hand icon to indicate direction would violate a cultural taboo in certain African cultures by representing a dismembered body part. Also, a pointing finger that indicates a hyperlink would be problematic too. A right arrow for the next page may mean previous page for Arabic and Hebrew language speakers as they read from left to right).
❑ Yes
❑ No
❑ Not applicable

Does the course use the full name for acronyms used in the body of the text?
❑ Yes
❑ No
❑ Not applicable
If *yes*, are the acronyms used for terms globally understood? (Note: Acronyms for terms such as identification numbers used in different parts of the world can be confusing to learners. Many countries of the world have identification or record keeping mechanisms for their citizens. For example, the United States government uses the acronym SSN for Social Security Number; the Canadian government uses the acronym SIN for Social Insurance Number, etc. Therefore, it will be problematic when a course offered by an US institution asks for a SSN number from non-US students.
  ❑ Yes
  ❑ No
  ❑ Not applicable

Could a student find the course to be discriminatory? (Note: It is difficult to judge on what may offend one person, but not another.)
❑ Yes
❑ No
❑ Not applicable
If *yes*, please describe:

Is the course culturally sensitive?
❑ Yes
❑ No
❑ Not applicable
❑ Not sure

Is the course sensitive to learners who come from an oral culture?
❑ Yes
❑ No
❑ Not applicable

Does the course promote cross-cultural interaction among students and instructor(s)?
❏ Yes
❏ No
❏ Not applicable

Is the course offered in multilingual format? (Note: Text in buttons or icons is harder to change. Hornett in an article written in 2000 entitled "Culturally Competent" advised us not to include text in graphics for e-learning content with the potential for being translated into other languages.)
❏ Yes
❏ No
❏ Not applicable
If *yes*, indicate the names of languages:

How does the course address cultural diversity from a learning perspective? (check all that apply):
❏ Course is tailored to specific cultures
❏ Course is designed to be culturally neutral
❏ Not applicable

Does the course use any icons, images, graphics, etc. which may have offensive meanings for learners of various cultures?
❏ Yes
❏ No
❏ Not applicable
❏ Not sure
Does the course vary the representation of concepts to allow for a multicultural audience?
❏ Yes
❏ No
❏ Not applicable

Does the course use terms or words that may not be used by the worldwide audience? (Note: People use the term "sidewalk" in the US and "pavement/footpath" in the UK. When such a term is needed, we should include both forms for a diverse audience, such as "students should use the sidewalk [or pavement] rather than trample the grass." The Website http://www.eurotexte.fr/translation/tips_brit_vs_amer.shtml provides some of the differences between American and British English.)
❏ Yes
❏ No
❏ Not applicable

Does the course use signs or symbols that may not be used by a worldwide audience?
- ❏ Yes
- ❏ No
- ❏ Not applicable

Does the course use symbolic and iconic representations that are not always commonly understood within one country? (Note: In South Africa, Kathy Murrell noted on the ITFORM listserve that the internationally recognized symbol of an escape exit is taken by nonliterate Zulu speaking people to mean "don't go there your hands, feet, and head will be cut off" - which makes sense when one looks closely at the image which has no neck, no wrist and no ankle.)
- ❏ Yes
- ❏ No
- ❏ Not applicable

Does the course use culture-specific analogies, metaphors, or expressions? (Note: For example, "Be sure to save your work frequently, remember *a stitch in time saves nine.")*
- ❏ Yes
- ❏ No
- ❏ Not applicable

Bias

Is the course sensitive to the biases of the authors of the content?
- ❏ Yes
- ❏ No
- ❏ Not applicable

Does the course present more than one viewpoint on controversial issues?
- ❏ Yes
- ❏ No
- ❏ Not applicable

Does the course designer try to eliminate any bias in the course content?
- ❏ Yes
- ❏ No
- ❏ Not applicable

Is the course content bias-free?
- ❏ Yes
- ❏ No

❑ Not applicable

Geographical Diversity

Is the course offered to geographically diverse populations?
❑ Yes
❑ No
❑ Not applicable
If *yes*, is the course sensitive about students from different time-zones (e.g.
synchronous communications are scheduled at reasonable times for all time zones
represented)?
    ❑ Yes
    ❑ No
    ❑ Not applicable

For assignment due dates, is the instructor sensitive to national and religious
holidays observed by students (not observed by the instructor)?
❑ Yes
❑ No
❑ Not applicable

Is the instructor sensitive about scheduling synchronous learning activities (such
as chat) during national and religious holidays observed by students (not observed
by the instructor)?
❑ Yes
❑ No
❑ Not applicable

Check if any of following issues are considered in scheduling online learning
activities? (check all that apply):
❑ Electrical power outages, load shading and circuit failure in some parts of the
    world may affect learners participating in online synchronous activities
❑ Electrical power outages, load shading and circuit failure in some parts of the
    world may prevent learners from submitting assignments on time
❑ Not applicable
❑ Other

Are the Internet connection fees a deterrent to participation in certain online
activities by learners? (Note: Learners who pay "by the minute" connection fees,
or long-distance charges may be affected by online discussion activities requiring
long connections times.)
❑ Yes
❑ No

❑ Not applicable
❑ Other

Learner Diversity

Does the institution conduct a survey to assess the learning style of the target population?
❑ Yes
❑ No
❑ Not applicable
❑ Other

Does the course provide flexibility to accommodate diverse learning styles?
❑ Yes
❑ No
❑ Not applicable

Is the course designed to have patience for learners who adapt to the distributed learning environment more slowly than others?
❑ Yes
❑ No
❑ Not applicable

Does the course allow students to remain anonymous during online discussions?
❑ Yes
❑ No
❑ Not applicable

Does the course foster mutual respect, tolerance, and trust? (Note: Such an environment depends on what the instructor and all learning support staff do during the course.)
❑ Yes
❑ No
❑ Not applicable

Does the course allow students to lurk during online *synchronous* discussions?
❑ Yes
❑ No
❑ Not applicable

Does the course allow students to lurk during online *asynchronous* discussions?
❑ Yes

❑ No
❑ Not applicable

Are participants required to assume roles or participate in scenarios that might be culturally and religiously offensive (Note: An e-learning course can ask learners to join in multi-person interactive worlds such as MOOs, MUDs and MUSHes to play and talk under a variety of personae. However, the topic and the roles that learners are asked to play may be culturally offensive. For instance, asking learners to play homosexual and bisexual characters in a MUD session may be ethically and religiously offensive to some learners.)
❑ Yes
❑ No
❑ Not applicable

Is the course designed to accommodate the needs of visually impaired learners?
❑ Yes
❑ No
❑ Not applicable
If *yes*, check all that apply:
    ❑ Learners can use "text-to-reader" software to participate in the course
    ❑ Other (specify)

Does the course offer an audio version for visually impaired learners?
❑ Yes
❑ No
❑ Not applicable

Digital Divide

Is the digital divide issue considered in designing the e-learning content?
❑ Yes
❑ No
❑ Not applicable
If *yes*, check all of the following measures that apply
    ❑ Only essential multimedia elements are used in the course to reduce bandwidth problem
    ❑ Multimedia elements (graphics, audio, video) are accompanied by text equivalents to be accessible by people with disabilities
    ❑ Other (specify)

Is the course sensitive to a diverse student population's accessibility to the Internet?
❑ Yes

❑ No
❑ Not applicable

Etiquette

Does the institution have etiquette guidelines?
❑ Yes
❑ No
❑ Not applicable

Does the course provide any guidance to learners on how to behave and post messages in online discussions so that their postings do not hurt others' feelings?
❑ Yes
❑ No
❑ Not applicable

If a student fails to follow the etiquette of the course more than one time, how does the instructor work with each student to promote compliance? (check all that apply):
❑ The student receives final notices with consequences
❑ The student is put on probation
❑ The student is penalize by lowering his/her grade or points
❑ The student is remove from the discussion forum
❑ Other
❑ Not applicable

Legal Issues

Does the course comply with the institution's policies and guidelines (if any) regarding all Web page development?
❑ Yes
❑ No
❑ Not applicable

Does the institution provide privacy policies and guidelines on online postings?
❑ Yes
❑ No
❑ Not applicable
If *yes*, does the course comply with the institution's privacy policies and guidelines for online postings?
❑ Yes

❑ No
❑ Not applicable

Does the course provide ethics policies that outline rules, regulations, guidelines, and prohibitions?
❑ Yes
❑ No
❑ Not applicable

Does the course get previous students' permission to use their online discussions postings or any other data that belong to them?
❑ Yes
❑ No
❑ Not applicable

Does the institution store students' text dialogs generated from mailing lists or computer conferencing exchanges?
❑ Yes
❑ No
❑ Not applicable
If *yes*, does it release students' text dialogs to others? (check all that apply):
    ❑ Yes, it releases students' text dialogs to other with students' permission
    ❑ Yes, it releases students' text dialogs to other without students' permission
    ❑ No
    ❑ Not applicable

Does the course provide institutional policies and guidelines regarding fraudulent activities in course-related testing, assignments and projects?
❑ Yes
❑ No
❑ Not applicable

Does the course clearly inform students about the consequences (e.g., in terms of course grade and academic status) of any forms of plagiarism?
❑ Yes
❑ No
❑ Not applicable
If *yes*, check all that apply:
    ❑ Receive a failing grade in the course
    ❑ Receive a failing grade on that particular paper
    ❑ Dismissal from the institution
    ❑ Name shows up on the list of cheaters in the institution
    ❑ Institution shares the student's cheating record with other academic institutions
    ❑ Other

Does the course provide a mini lesson on plagiarism?
❑ Yes
❑ No
❑ Not applicable
If *yes*, check all that apply:
    ❑ Learners identify an example of plagiarism
    ❑ Learners are advised how to cite or give credit to the source
    ❑ Other

Does the course require students to sign an agreement on plagiarism?
❑ Yes
❑ No
❑ Not applicable

Does the institution have a legal office where faculty members can get answers to legal matters concerning online courses?
❑ Yes
❑ No
❑ Not applicable
❑ Other (specify)

Check if the institution provides training sessions with up-to-date information on copyright issues relevant to e-learning? (check all that apply):

Role of Individual	Training Session Format			
	Online	*Face-to-Face*	*Other*	*Not Applicable*
Learner				
Instructor (full-time)				
Instructor (part-time)				
Trainer				
Trainer Assistant				
Tutor				
Technical Support				
Help Desk				
Librarian				
Counselor				
Graduate Assistant				
Administrator				
Project Manager				
Instructional Designer				
Graphic Artist				
Programmer				
Multimedia Developers				

Other (specify)				

Does the course acquire permission to use copyrighted information and materials from appropriate copyright holders?
- ❏ Yes
- ❏ No
- ❏ Not applicable

Does the course get students' permission to post any of the following on the Web? (check all that apply):

Student Materials	Permission			
	Yes	No	NA	Other
Students' projects				
Students' Webfolios				
Students' photographs				
Students' email addresses				
Students' telephone numbers				
Students' mailing address				
Other				

Does the course provide information about institutional policies and guidelines about copyrights?
- ❏ Yes
- ❏ No
- ❏ Not applicable
- ❏ Other (specify)

Does the course provide appropriate information about copyright laws concerning learning activities on the Internet?
- ❏ Yes
- ❏ No
- ❏ Not applicable

INTERFACE DESIGN

Page and Site Design

Check if Web pages look good in a variety of Web browsers and in text-based browsers, all recent versions of Internet Explorer and Netscape, and so on.

Browser	Best Viewed By (Type versions)	Not Best Viewed By (Type versions)
Netscape		
Explorer		

Check if the Web documents are available in any of the following formats? (check all that apply):
❑ PDF
❑ HTML
❑ XML
❑ Word processed
❑ Text file
❑ Not applicable
❑ Other (specify)

Does the course use the following interface structures? (check all that apply):
❑ Text/menu
❑ Graphical User Interface (GUI)
❑ Voice synthesis and recognition
❑ Not applicable
❑ Other (specify)

Does the course provide printable transcripts of any streaming audio and video used in the course?
❑ Yes
❑ No
❑ Not applicable
❑ Other

Do the following elements, if used, complement the textual content of the course? (check all that apply):
❑ Graphics
❑ Audio
❑ Video
❑ Animation
❑ None used

❑ Other (specify)

Do the pages of the course use reasonable blank or white spaces (about 20%) to help readers' eyes move through the content more easily and comfortably? (Note: Insufficient white space can contribute to cluttered screens.)
❑ Yes
❑ No
❑ Not applicable

Is the program attractive and appealing to the eye and ear? (Note: Remember that different people may find different colors or fonts appealing.)
❑ Yes
❑ No
❑ Not applicable
❑ Other

Is the text throughout the course legible?
❑ Yes
❑ No
❑ Not applicable

Throughout the course, are background colors of screens compatible with the foreground colors of the screens (so that they complement rather compete)?
❑ Yes
❑ No
❑ Not applicable

Does the site have a consistent look with the course print materials so the learner can easily make the connection between online course information and correspondence that comes in the mail?
❑ Yes
❑ No
❑ Not applicable

Does the course use a consistent font type across elements such as heading, body text, link, etc.?
❑ Yes
❑ No
❑ Not applicable

Does the course use a standard font type so that text appears the same in different computer platforms and browsers? (e.g., Arial, Times Roman, Helvetica fonts appear the same in different platforms. However, it is a client-side decision; users can display fonts however they want.)
❑ Yes

❏ No
❏ Not applicable

Does the course use a consistent layout including color and the placement of titles
and content on Web pages?
❏ Yes
❏ No
❏ Not applicable

Does the choice of graphics enhance the learners understanding of the site's
purpose?
❏ Yes
❏ No
❏ Not applicable

How fast do the pages on the course Website load? Do the screens load quickly?
Or, must the learner wait for large amounts of graphics, video, audio, and applets
to load? (Note: Large images and multimedia files require a long time to
download. However, loading speed may vary with users' Internet connection
speeds. The course should be designed to use bandwidth efficiently in order to
minimize learners' frustration. It is always a good idea to test pages at various
Internet connection speeds)
❏ Fast
❏ Fairly fast
❏ Somewhat slow
❏ Very slow

Do parts of the page appear even though the site is not fully loaded?
❏ Yes
❏ No
❏ Not applicable

Do the lessons, assignments and tests take a longer time to complete than the
course allow? (Note: It should not be a surprise to anyone that learners from
diverse geographical locations with varying Internet connection speeds may take
longer to complete learning activities on the Internet than the course designers
estimated. To avoid learners' dissatisfaction, course lessons and timed-quizzes or
assignments should be tested at dial-up speeds with a representative population.)
❏ Yes
❏ No
❏ Not applicable

Downloading audio and video is often time-consuming. Does the course assign
students pre-listening work or other instructional activities while the files are
downloading?

❑ Yes
❑ No
❑ Not applicable

Does the site use frames?
❑ Yes
❑ No
❑ Not applicable
If *yes*, does it also have a non-frames version available?
   ❑ Yes
   ❑ No
   ❑ Not applicable
   ❑ Other (specify)

Does the course give credit to individuals involved in designing and developing the course? (Note: This can be put under a menu item entitled "credit." A credit section is very useful to learners because it allows them to see the credentials of individuals who were involved in the creation of the course. Creditor recognition may not be appropriate for some sites including government and other settings.)

Course Team	Yes	No	NA	Other
Instructor				
Subject Matter Expert (SME) or Content Expert				
Instructional Designer				
Programmer				
Graphic Artist				
Multimedia Developer				
Course Manager				
Other (specify)				

Does the Website provide links to any of the following Websites within the institution? Check all that apply:
❑ Institution's Website
❑ Admissions Office
❑ Financial Aid Office
❑ Academic Departments
❑ Accounting Department
❑ Registrar's Office
❑ Student Services
❑ Student Organizations (Greek, Academic Clubs, etc.)
❑ Information Technology Services
❑ Professional Development
❑ Continuing Education
❑ Other (specify)

Does the course have a link to the instructor's home page and curriculum vitae?

❑ Yes
❑ No
❑ Not applicable

Are colored graphics, if used, clearly interpretable when printed in black and white? (Note: Some users like to print out Web pages to read them later. With a black and white printer, a variety of different colors used in a graphic to distinguish critical parts and functions may not be visible in the print out.)
❑ Yes
❑ No
❑ Not applicable

Does each screen of the course print one printer page?
❑ Yes
❑ No
❑ Not applicable

Content Design

Check if the course uses any of the following ways to gain learner attention? (check all that apply):
❑ Novelty
❑ Animation
❑ Motion (e.g., animated GIFs)
❑ Captioned graphics
❑ Changes in brightness
❑ Contrast between object of interest and its surroundings.
❑ Colors, sounds, and symbols that focus on specific content
❑ Other (specify)

Check if the course uses any of the following ways to improve learner retention? (check all that apply):
❑ Sequenced screens
❑ Meaningfully organized contents
❑ Overviews
❑ Consistent screen layout (consistent placement of title, graphic, textual contents, etc)
❑ Chunked materials, presenting together when appropriate
❑ Introductions and summaries
❑ Other (specify)

Does the course follow the "one idea per paragraph" rule?
❑ Yes

❑ No
❑ Not applicable

Is the text chunked and presented in a way that enables scanning and comprehension? (Note: Throughout the course headings and sub-headings should be parallel, short, and logically connected so that readers can scan them.)
❑ Yes
❑ No
❑ Not applicable

Check if any of the following multimedia presentation components are used in the course? (check all that apply):
❑ Text
❑ Graphics
❑ Animation
❑ Audio
❑ Video
❑ Other (specify)
If *yes*, does the mixture of multimedia components contribute to a rich learning environment?
    ❑ Yes
    ❑ No
    ❑ Not applicable

How effectively does the course use multimedia presentation components to create meaningful learning? (check all that apply):

Multimedia Components	Effectiveness			
	High	Moderate	Poor	Other
Text				
Graphics				
Animation				
Audio				
Video				
Other (specify)				

The course content is presented with proper (check all that apply):
❑ Grammar
❑ Punctuation
❑ Spelling
❑ Syntax (how words are put together to form phrases or sentences)
❑ Not applicable
❑ Other (specify)

The course content is presented with appropriate and relevant (check all that apply):

❑ Text
❑ Graphics
❑ Animation
❑ Audio
❑ Video
❑ Other (specify below)

Does the course provide an easy mechanism for electronic publishing for students and instructors?
❑ Yes
❑ No
❑ Not applicable

Navigation

Does the course provide structural aids (i.e., unit, lesson, activities, etc.) to help learners navigate the course?
❑ Yes
❑ No
❑ Not applicable
❑ Other (specify)

Does the course provide a site map (i.e., big picture of the course) to help learners navigate the course?
❑ Yes
❑ No
❑ Not applicable
❑ Other (specify)

To avoid bandwidth bottlenecks, does the course ask students to download large audio, video and graphic files to their hard drives before the instructional events?
❑ Yes
❑ No
❑ Not applicable
❑ Other (specify)

Do pages of the course fit within any graphical browser window without any horizontal or sideways scrolling? (Note: Sideways scrolling can be awkward and annoying at times. It seems to happen when tables are given widths in pixels instead of percentages; a given browser can be too small for the pixels required to display a page, but the percentage is defined as relative to the browser's width.)
❑ Yes
❑ No

❏ Not applicable

Are all links clearly labeled, and do they serve an easily identified purpose, so that learners have enough information to know whether they should click a link?
❏ Yes
❏ No
❏ Not applicable
❏ Other (specify)

Do users have the option to "skip" or "turn off" any animation or media components in the course? (Note: They can be part of the design, but it is a client-side decision too.)
❏ Yes
❏ No
❏ Not applicable
❏ Other (specify)

Does the site contain so many internal links as to be distracting?
❏ Yes
❏ No
❏ Not applicable

Does the site contain so many external links as to be distracting?
❏ Yes
❏ No
❏ Not applicable

Does the site use any icons that are difficult to remember? (Note: In using icons, we should ask "Is it clear what they represent? Does what they represent relate to what they do?")

❏ Yes
❏ No
❏ Not applicable
❏ Other (specify)

Does the course use a consistent color for both unvisited and visited links? (Note: The standard link colors such as 'blue' for unvisited links and 'reddish or purple' for visited links can be used on every page of the course site.)
❏ Yes
❏ No
❏ Not applicable
❏ Other (specify)

Is the course consistent with the use of terminology throughout? (Note: If you use a term or word on one Webpage, it is always wise to use the same term throughout the course.)

❑ Yes
❑ No
❑ Not applicable
❑ Other (specify)

Does the course indicate the size (e.g., 13k, 200k, etc.) of the multimedia files used?

❑ Yes
❑ No
❑ Not applicable
❑ Other (specify)

Does the course have structural flexibility by providing students the choice of multiple pathways through the instruction?

❑ Yes
❑ No
❑ Not applicable
❑ Other (specify)

Does the course offer suggested pathways for the user? (Note: Learners tend to follow links in the course. Therefore, hyperlinking in pages should be well-thought out as they suggest pathways for users.)

❑ Yes
❑ No
❑ Not applicable
❑ Other (specify)

How easy is it to navigate the course Website? (Can users move from page to page, and link to link with ease without getting lost or confused?)

❑ Very easy
❑ Fairly easy
❑ Somewhat difficult
❑ Very difficult

Is any part of the course linked to pages that are under construction? (Note: Avoid linking courses to incomplete sites.)

❑ Yes
❑ No
❑ Not applicable
❑ Other (specify)

Are learners informed when they use outside links that lead to different Websites? (Note: In his Distance Educational journal article in 1997, Boshier suggested using signposts or some visual guidance to expedite their return. However, if we open external sites in new browser windows, we do not need any signposts.)
- ❑ Yes
- ❑ No
- ❑ Not applicable
- ❑ Other (specify)

When a course contains links to sites located in different countries with different cultures (where navigation or expression icons may differ from the learners' native culture), are there any cues on how to adjust to unfamiliar navigation or a different instructional environment? (Boshier, 1997)
- ❑ Yes
- ❑ No
- ❑ Not applicable
- ❑ Other (specify)

Does the site include a search feature?
- ❑ Yes
- ❑ No
- ❑ Not applicable
- ❑ Other (specify)

If *yes*, check all that apply?
- ❑ Internal search feature within course Website
- ❑ External search feature

Does the course use consistent symbols and words as navigation aids? (Boshier, 1997)
- ❑ Yes
- ❑ No
- ❑ Not applicable
- ❑ Other (specify)

Does the course provide a support mechanism to indicate the progress made? (Note: For example, links that have been visited become a light red color - "bread-crumbing").
- ❑ Yes
- ❑ No
- ❑ Not applicable
- ❑ Other (specify)

Does the course include features such as context maintenance to automatically return a student to the point where he/she left off during the previous session?
- ❑ Yes

❑ No
❑ Not applicable
❑ Other (specify)

Does the course provide a progress map or calendar for students to measure their achievement?
❑ Yes
❑ No
❑ Not applicable
❑ Other (specify)

Check all options that apply about menus in the course:
❑ Menus are deep (i.e., more layers)
❑ Menus are shallow
❑ More choices should be available in the menus
❑ Should limit the number of choices in the menus
❑ Not applicable
❑ Other (specify)

Does every page of the course (where frames are not used) have links back to the site's main page?
❑ Yes
❑ No
❑ Not applicable
❑ Other (specify)

Are images used in the course stored on the course Website? (Note: Images saved in places other than the course site may slow down the loading time. Also, if the owner of the image removes it or changes its location, the image will not be found and the "broken image icon" will be displayed (Maddux, 1998).
❑ Yes
❑ No
❑ Not applicable
❑ Other (specify)

Do all the inside links in the course link to the correct locations?
❑ Yes
❑ No
❑ Not applicable
❑ Other (specify)

Do all the outside links in the course link to the correct locations?
❑ Yes
❑ No
❑ Not applicable

❑ Other (specify)

Does the course have any dead links (i.e. inactive links)?
❑ Yes
❑ No
❑ Not applicable
❑ Other (specify)
If *yes*, is there a system or mechanism to check the dead links that may exist within the course and update it on a regular basis?
 ❑ Yes
 ❑ No
 ❑ Not applicable
 ❑ Other (specify)
If yes, how often are dead links checked?
 ❑ Daily
 ❑ Weekly
 ❑ Monthly
 ❑ Quarterly
 ❑ Other (specify)

Does the course have a site that keeps users informed about any changes in URLs used in the course and other course relevant contents? (Note: For this book, a Website at http://BooksToRead.com/elearning/el-update.htm is maintained to inform readers regarding the change of addresses for chapter-related Websites and other corrections.)
❑ Yes
❑ No
❑ Not applicable

Does the course overuse hyperlinks in course pages?
❑ Yes
❑ No
❑ Not applicable

How is the quality of the streaming sound and video used in the course?

Streaming	Quality				
	Excellent	Good	Average	Poor	Very Poor
Sound					
Video					
Other (specify)					

Accessibility

Is the course Website designed to be accessible by a wider user population?
❏ Yes
❏ No
❏ Not applicable
❏ Other (specify)

Are various accessibility barriers considered in the design of the course? (Note: Web pages can be run through Bobby (http://bobby.cast.org) to test Web pages and help expose and repair barriers to accessibility and encourage compliance with existing accessibility guidelines, such as Section 508 and the W3C's WCAG.)
❏ Yes
❏ No
❏ Not applicable
❏ Other (specify)

Is the course Section-508 or W3C compliant?
❏ Yes
❏ No
❏ Not applicable
❏ Other (specify)
If so, at what level?

Does the course use alternate text for the images? (Note: The alternate text for all non-text elements can be read aloud by software for synthesizing speech, and is therefore, essential for visually impaired learners.)
❏ Yes
❏ No
❏ Not applicable

Does the course provide captions for audio content? (Note: People who cannot hear can read the audio content from the captions.)
❏ Yes
❏ No
❏ Not applicable

Can various screens of the course be resized to accommodate low-vision users? (Note: Even if the Web pages are designed to a specific screen size, the user can easily resize the screen by using the maximize or minimize option in the browser.)
❏ Yes
❏ No
❏ Not applicable

Are all the colors used in the various screens of the course clearly distinguishable by the visually impaired?
❑ Yes
❑ No
❑ Not applicable

Can users who cannot use the mouse navigate through the e-learning materials using the keyboard instead?
❑ Yes
❑ No
❑ Not applicable
❑ Other (specify)

Does the course use acronyms? (Note: It is always helpful to have full name represented by the acronym used the first time appears in the text. For example, UTC (Universal Coordinated Time). Some link acronyms to a glossary sites, however, it is an extra step for users including individuals with disabilities. E-learning designers should use appropriate scripts in e-learning documents to embed the full name represented by the acronym.)
❑ Yes
❑ No
❑ Not applicable
❑ Other (specify)
If *yes*, check measure(s) taken to solve issues associated with acronyms and accessibility for individuals with disabilities? (check all that apply):
    ❑ Uses full name represented by the acronym the first time it appears in text
    ❑ Links to glossary
    ❑ Other (specify)

Usability Testing

Has there been a trial run beforehand with representative users?
❑ Yes
❑ No
❑ Not applicable
❑ Other (specify)

Do users find answers to the most frequently asked questions on the course site within a reasonable amount of time?
❑ Yes
❑ No
❑ Not applicable

Can users easily know where they are and navigate the site without guessing?
❑ Yes
❑ No
❑ Not applicable

Does the course use easy-to-understand terminology?
❑ Yes
❑ No
❑ Not applicable

Can learners easily take a look at or sample each part of the course? (Boshier, 1997)
❑ Yes
❑ No
❑ Not applicable

Is the site designed so that learners can easily get to a specific piece of content (in no more than 3 clicks)?
❑ Yes
❑ No
❑ Not applicable

RESOURCE SUPPORT

Online Support

Check if the course provides any of the following informational and communication options for any of the following individual(s)/office(s). (check all that apply):

Role of Individual	Method of Communication				
	Email	Live Chat	Telephone		Other
			Regular*	Toll free**	
Course Coordinator					
Instructor					
Tutor					
Graduate Assistant					
Discussion Facilitator/Moderator					
Copyright Coordinator					
Guest speaker (or outside expert)					
Counselor					
Career counseling services					
Technical support					
Learning resources					
Tutoring service					
Library services					
Admission office					
Registration service					
Bursar office					
Financial aid					
Bookstore					
Other					

* Should always include the area code with the telephone number

**If an institution decides to provide toll free phone call services for learners, then it must be available to all learners regardless of their diverse locations. For example, a US institution offering e-learning courses to learners worldwide should provide alternatives to toll free phone call such as 1-800, 1-877 or 1-866 to learners outside of the USA and Canada. Please note that 1-800 or 1-877 does not work outside the USA and Canada. Also, TTY phone services should be available for the deaf or the hearing impaired.

Does the course include a Frequently Asked Question (FAQ) page?
❑ Yes

❏ No
❏ Not applicable

Does the institution conduct a pre-assessment survey to identify if learners have the necessary skills for online learning?
❏ Yes
❏ No
❏ Not applicable

Is there an *introduction to online* or a similar course offered by the institution that covers any of the following skills? Check all that apply:

Skills	Yes	No	NA	Comment
Study skills (reading and writing guides, note taking, etc.)				
Self-discipline				
Time management				
Stress management				
Health and wellness				
Test anxieties				
How to use available resources				
Other				

Check if the course provides counseling sessions for distance learners by any of the following informational and communication options. (check all that apply):

Counseling Issues	Method of Communication									
	Face-to-Face Meeting (Hours Per Week)				Telephone (Hours Per Week)				E-Mail	Other
	1-3	4-6	7-10	Other	1-3	4-6	7-10	Other		
Guidance on study skills										
Time management										
Stress management and personal problems										
Career guidance										
Other (specify)										

Are students required to submit a Counseling Appointment Request Form (CARP) to the counselor prior to a counseling session? (Note: At the Athabasca University in Canada, students are required to complete and submit a CARP to request a session with counselor. Students are informed of the confirmation of appointments via e-mail within 7 business days.)
❏ Yes

❏ No
❏ Not applicable

Does the course provide any guidance to students on how to organize for online learning?
❏ Yes
❏ No
❏ Not applicable

Does the instructor assist students who encounter problems in completing their assignments?
❏ Yes
❏ No
❏ Not applicable

Do students receive guidance on any of the following skill(s)?
❏ Yes
❏ No
❏ Not applicable
If *yes*, check all that apply:
    ❏ Ability to work alone
    ❏ Ability to learn without face-to-face classroom interaction
    ❏ Ability to do collaborative work with never-met individuals
    ❏ Not applicable
    ❏ Other

Does the instructor/staff contact students (who fail to participate in regular online learning activities for the course) to see if they are encountering problems?
❏ Yes
❏ No
❏ Not applicable
If *yes*, how are students contacted? Check all that apply:
    ❏ E-mail
    ❏ Phone
    ❏ Fax
    ❏ Letter
    ❏ Other

Does the course provide any information or ideas about how many hours (approximately) per week students are expected to spend on course assignments?
❏ Yes
❏ No
❏ Not applicable

Do students receive any guidance on how to search course relevant resources on the Web using search engines?
❑ Yes
❑ No
❑ Not applicable

Do students receive any guidance on the quality and reliability of online resources they find using search engines?
❑ Yes
❑ No
❑ Not applicable

Does the course provide someone other than the instructor who can assist with student problems regarding learning tasks? (Note: In addition to the instructional team, the course can use peer-to-peer groups for such situations.)
❑ Yes
❑ No
❑ Not applicable
If *yes*, please specify

Does the instructor provide timely responses to student queries?
❑ Yes
❑ No
❑ Not applicable

Does the course provide someone other than the instructor who can help students with problems?
❑ Yes
❑ No
❑ Not applicable

Does the institution regularly review the effectiveness of counseling services?
❑ Yes
❑ No
❑ Not applicable
❑ Other (specify)
If *yes*, check if any of the following used for collecting data. (check all the apply):
  ❑ Student surveys
  ❑ Email communications
  ❑ Telephone
  ❑ Other (specify)

Does the course provide links to Websites that provide subject-related job postings? (Note: Jones International University provides students with links to Websites where they can either post their resume online or review job postings

from companies around the country (*http://www.e-globallibrary.com/eprise/main/egloballibrary/demo/index*).
❑   Yes
❑   No
❑   Not applicable
❑   Other (specify)

Check if the course provides technical support for distance learners by any of the following informational and communication options. (check all that apply):

Days	Method of Communication									
	Telephone (Hours)				Live Chat (Hours)				E-Mail	Other
	1-3	*4-6*	*7-10*	*Other*	*1-3*	*4-6*	*7-10*	*Other*		
Monday										
Tuesday										
Wednesday										
Thursday										
Friday										
Saturday										
Sunday										

Does the course provide troubleshooting (or expert technical support from specialized staff) assistance or a help line? (Note: If the course is hosted on a vendor's LMS (learning management system), then it needs to be very clearly described to learners about who provides the technical support for the LMS.)
❑   Yes
❑   No
❑   Not applicable

Does the course provide round-the-clock (24/7) technical support?
❑   Yes
❑   No
❑   Not applicable

If the course is offered in multiple languages, are the round-the-clock (24/7) technical support services available in all these languages?
❑   Yes
❑   No
❑   Not applicable

Does the course provide clear guidelines to the learners on what support can and cannot be expected from a help line? (Note: For example, things the student is responsible for, and things that the student can expect the help line to solve.)
❑   Yes

❑ No
❑ Not applicable

Do students receive any guidance on how to set up hardware equipment for desktop video conferencing (if needed for the course)?
❑ Yes
❑ No
❑ Not applicable

Does the course provide a print-based User Guide for learners?
❑ Yes
❑ No
❑ Not applicable

Do students receive any guidance on how to do the following?
❑ Send and respond to e-mail
❑ Send e-mail attachments
❑ Open files in e-mail
❑ Install required software
❑ Scan a picture
❑ Print within Webpage frames
❑ Create an online presentation using presentation software
❑ Transfer and receive files between the learner's desktop and the institution's server
❑ Organize bookmarks in the browser
❑ Other (specify)

Does the course provide technical support materials on the Web?
❑ Yes
❑ No
❑ Not applicable

Does technical support send e-mail answers to a question from one student about a general technical issue to all students?
❑ Yes
❑ No
❑ Not applicable

Check if any of the following forms of technical support are available for students (check all that apply):
❑ Help-desk technician on duty
❑ Interactive training video (online)
❑ Interactive training video (mailed to learners)
❑ Call-in lines
❑ Assistance from instructor/tutors

❑ Other
❑ Not applicable

If asynchronous help is provided, then how soon can learners expect to get answers to their e-mail, phone message, or fax inquiries from the Technical Support Staff?
❑ Within 6 hours
❑ Within 12 hours
❑ Within 24 hours
❑ Within 36 hours
❑ Within 48 hours
❑ Does not respond to e-mail messages
❑ Does not return phone messages
❑ Does not respond to fax messages
❑ Not applicable
❑ Other (specify)

In case of technical difficulties, what other ways can students submit their assignments?
❑ Fax
❑ Mail
❑ E-Mail attachment
❑ Not applicable
❑ Other (specify below)

Online Resources

Online Resources	Examples
Multimedia archives	Multimedia Educational Resource for Learning and Online Teaching (MERLOT) is a free and open resource designed primarily for faculty and students of higher education. Links to online learning materials are collected along with annotations such as peer reviews and assignments. URL: http://www.merlot.org
Mailing lists and their archives	Anyone can subscribe (generally at no charge) to an e-mail mailing list on a particular subject or subjects and to post messages. The Distance Education Online Symposium Listserv (DEOS-L) is a moderated listserv that facilitates discussion of current issues in distance education. URL: http://www.ed.psu.edu/acsde/deos/deos-l/deosl.asp
Frequently Asked	Hillsborough Community College in Florida hosts an e-learning

Questions (FAQs)	FAQs site for students. URL: http://www.hcc.cc.fl.us/dislearn/Summer_2003/studfaqs.htm
Glossaries	PlasmaLink Web Services provides the Glossary of Instructional Strategies as a resource for all educators. URL: http://glossary.plasmalink.com/glossary.html
e-books	The University of Virginia's E-Book Library has hundreds of publicly-available ebooks for classic British and American fiction, major authors, children's literature, American history, Shakespeare, African-American documents, the Bible, and much more. URL: http://etext.lib.virginia.edu/ebooks/ebooklist.html
Dictionaries	The Resources for the Study of Norwegian site provides online dictionaries in Norwegian and other languages. URL: http://employees.csbsju.edu/tnichol/norwegian.html#dict
Calculator	State University of New York developed an Online Calculator for prospective students to determine how much money they can save by taking a college-course from their home. URL: http://sln.suny.edu/sln/public/original.nsf/a6b56cc3058e682485256c790066b2d5?OpenForm
Webliographies	The Maritime History Webliography at the University of North Carolina attempts to organize and classify those resources currently available on the internet with some connection to maritime history. URL: http://www.ils.unc.edu/maritime/mhiweb/webhome.shtml
Recommended reading lists	A recommended reading list for educational technology, instructional technology, training, distance education, online learning, online education, open learning design, k-12, multimedia and user interface design. Also, contains Top Ten List by experts in the field. URL: http://BooksToRead.com/et.htm
Digital libraries	Institutions with online programs should consider either establishing their own digital libraries, partnership (consortia) digital libraries, or service agreement with other digital libraries to provide digital library support to their online students. These digital libraries should be created to insure that all available resources are complete, highly searchable and richly formatted (Schmitz, 2001). The California Digital Library (CDL) is an additional "co-library" of the University of California (UC) campuses, with a focus on digital materials and services. CDL is a collaborative effort of the ten UC campuses. URL: http://www.cdlib.org/
Computer	The Department of Sociology at University of California (Davis)

tutorials	developed a computer tutorial entitled "Add a Network Printer." URL: http://sociology.ucdavis.edu/tutorials/Add_a_Network_Printer_vie wlet_swf.html
Experts online	Experts Online hosted by the Local Initiatives Support Corporation is an interactive forum for professional discussion among industry experts, as well as national and local practitioners. Experts Online live event (free of charge) as a support and training service to community development practitioners nationwide. URL: http://www.liscnet.org/resources/experts_index.shtml
Journals and Magazines	*The Technology Source* (ISSN 1532-0030), a peer-reviewed bimonthly periodical published by the Michigan Virtual University, provides thoughtful, illuminating articles that will assist educators as they face the challenge of integrating information technology tools into teaching and into managing educational organizations. URL: http://ts.mivu.org/
Newsletters	The *LD OnLine Newsletter* provides up-to-date information for the field of learning disabilities. UR L: http://www.ldonline.org/subscribe.html
Newspapers	The Internet Public Library has links to online newspapers from around the world. URL: http://www.ipl.org/div/news/
Personal journals (i.e., Web logs or blogs)	Blogs or Weblogs an informal personal Websites which can be used as powerful e-learning resources. Weblogs are sometimes called Web journals. An increasing number of people are blogging every day. Therefore, there are numerous Weblogs in various topics which are updated regularly. Professor Ray Schroeder at the University of Illinois at Springfield scans the news daily for items of relevance in the field of new communication technologies, educational technologies, and online learning. He created three Weblogs (Online Learning Update, Education Technology, and Techno-News) to keep his technologies seminars and classes up-to-date and fresh for his students. URL: http://people.uis.edu/rschr1/bloggerinfo.html
Knowledge management	The Website entitled "Teaching and Implementing Knowledge Management Programs" provides many examples of companies and organizations that are implementing knowledge management. URL: http://www.icasit.org/kmclass/teaching/

Does the course have (or links to) any of the following online resources? (check all that apply):
❑ Multimedia archives

- ❑ Mailing lists and their archives
- ❑ Newsgroups
- ❑ FAQs
- ❑ Glossaries
- ❑ e-books
- ❑ Dictionaries
- ❑ Calculators
- ❑ Webliographies
- ❑ Recommended reading lists
- ❑ Databases
- ❑ Digital libraries
- ❑ Computer tutorials
- ❑ Experts online
- ❑ Electronic books
- ❑ Journals
- ❑ Magazines
- ❑ Newsletters
- ❑ Newspapers
- ❑ Documents
- ❑ Personal journals (i.e., web logs or blogs)
- ❑ Knowledge management

Are all available resources organized logically with course relevant categories?
- ❑ Yes
- ❑ No
- ❑ Not applicable

Do all categories of available online resources have brief descriptions about their contents?
- ❑ Yes
- ❑ No
- ❑ Not applicable

Does the course have a searchable *course glossary*?
- ❑ Yes
- ❑ No
- ❑ Not applicable

Does the course glossary include acronyms?
- ❑ Yes
- ❑ No
- ❑ Not applicable

Does the course provide an online bookstore (i.e. a means of purchasing course books online)?

❏ Yes
❏ No
❏ Not applicable
❏ Other (specify below)

Does the course provide access to other sources of information related to the course content (e.g. video, audio materials)?
❏ Yes
❏ No
❏ Not applicable
If *yes*, please describe:

Does the course provide summaries and reviews of online discussions?
❏ Yes
❏ No
❏ Not applicable

Does the course provide links to a variety of search engines?
❏ Yes
❏ No
❏ Not applicable

Does the course have any examples of course-related professional work available at other Websites?
❏ Yes
❏ No
❏ Not applicable

Are the external links to resources appropriately related to the context of the content?
❏ Yes
❏ No
❏ Not applicable

Do the external links to resources increase the credibility of the course?
❏ Yes
❏ No
❏ Not applicable

Are the external links checked on a regular basis to make sure they still work?
❏ Yes
❏ No
❏ Not applicable

Does the course provide a student annotation facility for students to make notes for future reference?

❑ Yes
❑ No
❑ Not applicable

Does the course make use of EPSS - Electronic Performance Support System (software designed to improve productivity by providing immediate on the job access to learning and information) as a research tool?

❑ Yes
❑ No
❑ Not applicable

Does the course provide examples of previous students' work on the Web?

❑ Yes
❑ No
❑ Not applicable

If *yes*, select all that apply and circle whether searchable and browsable:

    ❑ Projects (searchable browsable)
    ❑ Papers (searchable browsable)
    ❑ Text dialogue from discussion forums (searchable browsable)
    ❑ Text dialogue from online conferencing exchanges (searchable browsable)
    ❑ Other

Does the institution's library have library resources online?

❑ Yes
❑ No
❑ Not applicable

If *yes*, do students have access to its databases via the Internet or other network?

    ❑ Yes
    ❑ No
    ❑ Not applicable

Does the institution have an on-line means of borrowing books and other resources?

❑ Yes
❑ No
❑ Not applicable

If *yes*, describe the following:

    ❑ How long books or other resources can be kept
    ❑ How books or other resources can be returned (e.g., via regular mail or other means)

Does the institution have a digital library of its own?

❑ Yes
❑ No
❑ Not applicable

If *no*, does the institution have a partnership with other institutions to use their digital libraries?

    ❑ Yes
    ❑ No
    ❑ Not applicable
    ❑ Other (specify)

Do the online resource Websites provide bibliographies or lists of references to indicate the original sources of materials included in their sites?

❑ Yes
❑ No
❑ Not applicable
❑ Other (specify)

Check if students have access to any of the following: (Check all that apply):

❑ Online catalogs
❑ Periodical indexes
❑ Bibliographic databases
❑ Other

Check if the institution provides a special librarian who is available to assist learners at a distance using any of the following informational and communication options. (Note: AskUsNow is a live online interactive library service provided through a partnership of Maryland public, academic, and special libraries. Students can ask questions to librarians about their research in real time via the Internet—24 hours a day, seven days a week. URL: http://www.askusnow.info/) (check all that apply):

Days	Method of Communication									
	Telephone (Hours)				Live Chat (Hours)				E-Mail	Other
	1-3	*4-6*	*7-10*	*Other*	*1-3*	*4-6*	*7-10*	*Other*		
Monday										
Tuesday										
Wednesday										
Thursday										
Friday										
Saturday										
Sunday										

Does the institution make special arrangements with local libraries for distance learners to have access to library resources?

❑ Yes

❑ No
❑ Not applicable

Do remote students receive special training on how to access library resources electronically (e.g., library orientation)?
❑ Yes
❑ No
❑ Not applicable

Do bandwidth limitations affect remote access to library resources?
❑ Yes
❑ No
❑ Not applicable

Does the course provide an on-line course reference manual for site mechanics (how to use the site)?
❑ Yes
❑ No
❑ Not applicable

If needed for the coursework, does the course provide on-line tools such as a calculator for students to use?
❑ Yes
❑ No
❑ Not applicable

Does the institution have a knowledge management (KM) site?
❑ Yes
❑ No
❑ Not applicable

Does the course use Weblogs as resources for learning?
❑ Yes
❑ No
❑ Not applicable

Offline Resources

Does the course require any of the following off-line resources?
❑ Yes
❑ No
❑ Not applicable
If *yes*, check all that apply:

❑ Dictionaries
❑ Glossaries
❑ Books
❑ e-books
❑ Papers
❑ Maps
❑ .pdf files which can be downloaded for later reading
❑ Other (specify below)

Does the course require off-line reading assignments?
❑ Yes
❑ No
❑ Not applicable
If *yes*, how is the reading material accessed?

Does the host institution's library have a system of getting books and other materials for distance students via interlibrary loan?
❑ Yes
❑ No
❑ Not applicable

Does the institution provide information on how to get region-wide borrowers cards to borrow books from other academic libraries?
❑ Yes
❑ No
❑ Not applicable

Does the library fax documents to students?
❑ Yes
❑ No
❑ Not applicable

EVALUATION

Evaluation of the E-Learning Content Development Process

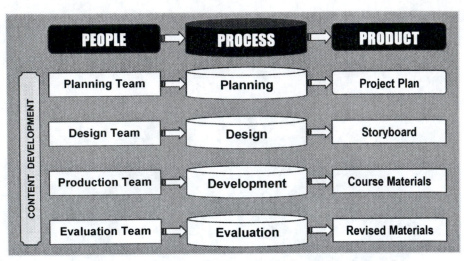

Figure 1. People-Process-Product Continuum for the Content Development Process

Check the overall *performance of individuals* involved in the various stages of the content development process. (check all that apply):

Role of Individual	Name of Person	Content Development Stages															
		Planning				Design				Production				Evaluation			
		Excellent	Good	Fair	Poor	Excellent	Good	Fair	Poor	Excellent	Good	Fair	Poor	Excellent	Good	Fair	Poor
Director																	
Project Manager																	
Business Developer																	
Consultant / Advisor																	
Research and Design Coordinator																	
Content or Subject Matter Expert																	

Instructional Designer																			
Interface Designer																			
Copyright Coordinator																			
Evaluation Specialist																			
Production Coordinator																			
Course Integrator																			
Programmer																			
Editor																			
Graphic Artist																			
Multimedia Developer																			
Photographer / Videographer (cameraman)																			
Learning Objects Specialist																			
Quality Assurance																			
Pilot Subjects																			

Check the *performance level of the management* team in managing the e-learning projects. (check all that apply):

Skill Types	Management Team														
	Director					Project Manager					Other				
	Excellent	Good	Fair	Poor	NA	Excellent	Good	Fair	Poor	NA	Excellent	Good	Fair	Poor	NA
Recruiting															
Supervising															
Budgeting															
Planning															
Scheduling															
Assigning tasks to team members															
Interpersonal															
Presentation															
Technological															
Research															
Outsourcing projects components															

Tracking project progress														
Conducting meetings														
Oral communication														
Written Communication														
Consensus building														
Conflict resolution														
Ability to work with others on a team														
Other (specify)														

Rate the performance level of the various *stages of the content development* process:

Content Development Stage	Performance					
	Excellent	Good	Fair	Poor	NA	Comments
Planning						
Design						
Production						
Evaluation						

Rate the performance level of the various *types of evaluation* process:

Evaluation Type	Performance					
	Excellent	Good	Fair	Poor	NA	Comments
Content Review						
Rapid Prototype						
Alpha Class						
Beta Class						
Other (specify)						

Rate the performance level of the following *tools* and *services* used during the content development process:

Tools and Services	Performance					
	Excellent	Good	Fair	Poor	NA	Comments
Content Development /Authoring Tool						
Learning Management System						
Screen Reader Software						
Accessibility Evaluation Tool						

Network Server						
Hardware Vendor Services						
Software Vendor Services						
Postal Delivery Services						
Other (specify)						

Rate the performance level of the following sites:

Site	Performance					
	Excellent	Good	Fair	Poor	NA	Comments
Development Site						
Project Support Site						
Knowledge Management Site						
Other (specify)						

Rate the *products* of the various stages of the e-learning content development process.

Stages	Product Type	Product Quality					
		Excellent	Good	Fair	Poor	NA	Comments
Planning	• *Project Plan*						
	•						
	•						
	•						
Design	• *Storyboard*						
	•						
	•						
	•						
Production	• *Course Materials*						
	•						
	•						
	•						
Evaluation	• *Revised Materials*						
	•						
	•						
	•						

Evaluation of the E-Learning Environment

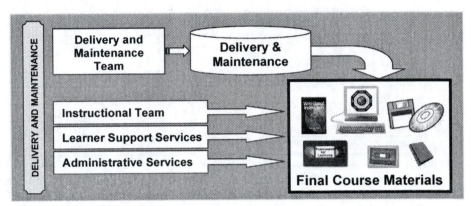

Figure 2. People-Process-Product Continuum for the Delivery and Maintenance Process

Rate the overall performance of the individuals involved in the delivery and maintenance stages of e-learning. (check all that apply):

Role of Individual	Name of Individual	Performance Level									
		Delivery Stage					Maintenance Stage				
		Excellent	Good	Fair	Poor	NA	Excellent	Good	Fair	Poor	NA
Project Manager											
Delivery Coordinator											
Systems Administrator											
Server/Database Programmer											
Other (specify)											

Rate the performance of security measures in the course:
- ❏ Excellent
- ❏ Good
- ❏ Fair
- ❏ Poor
- ❏ Not applicable

Rate the overall performance of individuals involved in the instructional stage. (check all that apply):

Role of Individual (Instructional Team)	Individual Name	Performance					
		Excellent	Good	Fair	Poor	NA	Comments
Online Course Coordinator							
Instructor (or Trainer)							
Instructor Assistant							
Tutor							
Discussion Facilitator/Moderator							
Learning Objects Specialist							
Copyright Coordinator							
Guest Speaker (or outside Expert)							
Other (specify)							

How are instructor's written communication skills?
- ❑ Excellent
- ❑ Good
- ❑ Fair
- ❑ Poor

How are the instructor's oral communication skills?
- ❑ Excellent
- ❑ Good
- ❑ Fair
- ❑ Poor

How is the instructor's or trainer's level of enthusiasm in teaching the course?
- ❑ Excellent
- ❑ Good
- ❑ Fair
- ❑ Poor

Rate the instructor's or trainer's performance in promoting online interaction in the course?
- ❑ Excellent
- ❑ Good
- ❑ Fair

❑ Poor
❑ Not applicable

Rate the overall performance of the learner support staff involved in the instructional stage. (check all that apply):

Role of Individual (Learner Support)	Individual Name	Performance					
		Excellent	Good	Fair	Poor	NA	Comments
Technical Support Specialist							
Library Services							
Counseling Services							
Customer Service							
Other (specify)							

Rate the overall performance of the administrative support services. (check all that apply):

Administrative Support	Performance					
	Excellent	Good	Fair	Poor	NA	Comments
Admission						
Registration						
Payment						
Bookstore						
Financial Aid						
Other (specify)						

Evaluation of E-Learning at the Program and Institutional Levels

Check if the institution or program has an online evaluation method (e.g., evaluation forms) in place to evaluate the performance of any of the following individuals and support services. (Note: Since several entities such as people, tools, and resources are involved in an e-learning course, the institution should develop evaluation instruments encompassing these entities. There can be a single evaluation instrument for each individual or a combined evaluation instrument for the course, program, and institution.) Check all that apply:

Individual and Support Services	Online Evaluation Method Available?			
	Yes	No	NA	Other
Director				
Project				
Business Developer				
Consultant / Advisor				
Research and Design Coordinator				
Content or Subject Matter Expert				
Instructional Designer				
Interface Designer				
Copyright Coordinator				
Evaluation Specialist				
Production Coordinator				
Course Integrator				
Programmer				
Editor				
Graphic Artist				
Multimedia Developer				
Photographer/Videographer				
Learning Objects Specialist				
Quality Assurance				
Pilot Subjects				
Delivery Coordinator				
Systems Administrator				
Server/Database Programmer				
Online Course Coordinator				
Instructor(or Trainer)				
Instructor Assistant				
Tutor				
Discussion Facilitator/Moderator				
Customer Service				
Technical Support Specialist				
Library Services				
Counseling Services				
Administrative Services				
Registration Services				
Marketing				
Other (specify)				

Check the status of the accreditation review by accrediting agencies:

Name of Accreditation Agency	Review Status	
	Satisfactory	Unsatisfactory

Rate the performance of e-learning marketing by the institution:
❑ Excellent
❑ Good
❑ Fair
❑ Poor
❑ Not applicable

Rate the effectiveness of institution's e-learning partnerships with other institutions:
❑ Excellent
❑ Good
❑ Fair
❑ Poor
❑ Not applicable

Does the course use an instant feedback button on most screens/pages in order to receive learners' feedback for improvement of the course?
❑ Yes
❑ No
❑ Not applicable

Does the course have an archive of previous students' evaluations of the course? (Note: Most online courses are modified/updated every semester based on new content and students' evaluation. Therefore, previous students' evaluation reports can sometimes be irrelevant and misleading. Professor Christopher Dede of the Learning and Teaching program at the Harvard University posts students evaluations from the previous semester.
URL: http://www.gse.harvard.edu/~dedech/502/T-5022.pdf)
❑ Yes
❑ No
❑ Not applicable

Is the course peer-reviewed during its design and development process by the following individuals? Check all that apply:
❑ Other online instructors within the institution
❑ Peers in the field
❑ Outside consultant
❑ Not applicable
❑ Other (specify)

Does the course conduct pilot testing with the target population?
❑ Yes
❑ No
❑ Not applicable

Does the course offer students an opportunity to give feedback to the institution about the quality and benefits/disadvantages of the course?
- ❏ Yes
- ❏ No
- ❏ Not applicable

Does the institution conduct regular surveys to find out about student satisfaction with the course?
- ❏ Yes
- ❏ No
- ❏ Not applicable

Do students recommend the course to others?
- ❏ Yes
- ❏ No
- ❏ Not applicable

Are course materials reviewed semesterly (or quaterly) to ensure their quality?
- ❏ Yes
- ❏ No
- ❏ Not applicable

If *yes*, check all that apply:
- ❏ Peer reviewed by colleagues
- ❏ Reviewed by the program coordinator
- ❏ Reviewed by the department chair
- ❏ Reviewed by the dean
- ❏ Reviewed by the course review committee
- ❏ Other (please describe below)

Does anyone in the institution (e.g., program director, department chairman, or training manager) review transcripts of instructor's feedback in online facilitation to evaluate his or her performance?
- ❏ Yes
- ❏ No
- ❏ Not applicable
- ❏ Other (specify)

Is the learning environment interactive? (Note: A well-designed learning environment should provide interactive experiences for it various learning tasks. When learners are engaged, they learn and enjoy.)
- ❏ Yes
- ❏ No
- ❏ Not applicable

Does the institution keep a record of learner completion rates every time the course is offered?

❑ Yes
❑ No
❑ Not applicable
❑ Other (specify)

Rate the quality of e-learning orientation sessions (provided by the institution) for the following stakeholder groups? (check all that apply):

Role of Individual	Quality				
	Excellent	Good	Fair	Poor	NA
Students					
Instructor					
Trainer					
Facilitator					
Tutor					
Technical Support					
Help Desk					
Librarian					
Counselor					
Facilitator					
Administrative Staff					
Other (specify)					

How effective was the technology infrastructure for the course?

❑ Very effective
❑ Moderately effective
❑ Not effective
❑ Not applicable
❑ Other

Assessment of Learners

How are the learners assessed during the course? Check all that apply:

❑ Pre-test
❑ Post-test
❑ Diagnostic test
❑ Topical/Research Paper
❑ Group Projects
❑ Individual Project
❑ Online Presentation
❑ Assignments
❑ Proctored online tests
❑ Proctored written tests

❑ Portfolio development
❑ Case studies
❑ Lab report
❑ Journal (Web logs or blogs)
❑ Not applicable
❑ Other (specify)

Are assignment types selected for the course appropriate for the content types?
❑ Yes
❑ No
❑ Not applicable
❑ Other (specify)

Check if any of the following test formats are used in the course:
❑ Multiple choice
❑ True/false
❑ Fill-in-the blanks
❑ Short Answer
❑ Essay questions
❑ Randomized quizzes
❑ Timed quizzes
❑ Quizzes with possible retries
❑ Scoring online
❑ Score analysis
❑ Score reporting online
❑ Not applicable
❑ Other (specify)

Rate the appropriateness of the test *format* for each learning objective:

Lesson	Objective	Number of Test Items					Length of Test Items				
		Excellent	Good	Fair	Poor	NA	Excellent	Good	Fair	Poor	NA
1	1										
	2										
	3										
	4										
	5										
	6										
	7										
	8										
2	1										
	2										
	3										
	4										
	5										
	6										
	7										

	8										
3	1										
	2										
	3										
	4										
	5										
	6										
	7										
	8										

Rate the adequacy of the *number* and *length* of test items in each learning objective:

Lesson	**Objective**	**Number of Test Items**					**Length of Test Items**				
		Excellent	Good	Fair	Poor	NA	Excellent	Good	Fair	Poor	NA
1	1										
	2										
	3										
	4										
	5										
	6										
	7										
	8										
2	1										
	2										
	3										
	4										
	5										
	6										
	7										
	8										
3	1										
	2										
	3										
	4										
	5										
	6										
	7										
	8										

Does the assessment provide students with the opportunity to demonstrate what they have learned in the course?
❑ Yes
❑ No
❑ Not applicable

Does the course provide students with clear grading criteria?
❑ Yes
❑ No

❑ Not applicable
❑ Other (specify)

What is the timeline for the instructor to provide feedback on assignments? (Note: The feedback timeline will depend on the type of assignment.)
❑ Immediate
❑ Within a week of the assignment's receipt
❑ Within two weeks of the assignment's receipt
❑ Within a month of the assignment's receipt
❑ Open time
❑ Not applicable

Does the course give sufficient time for student to complete course assignments?
❑ Yes
❑ No
❑ Not applicable (e.g., self-paced)

Does the course require students to log on to the course Website during certain periods of time (e.g., at least once a week) as proof of their attendance?
❑ Yes
❑ No
❑ Not applicable
If *yes*, does the instructor or facilitator contact the absent students?
　❑ Yes
　❑ No
　❑ Not applicable

Does the course require students to participate in online discussions?
❑ Yes
❑ No
❑ Not applicable
If *yes*, how (check all that apply):
　❑ By responding to main discussion topics/questions posted by the instructor or facilitator
　❑ By responding to other students' posting for the original topic/question
　❑ Other

Does the course clearly explain how a student's discussion participation contributes toward a student's grade?
❑ Yes
❑ No
❑ Not applicable

Are the quizzes/tests in this course accurate and fair?
❑ Yes

❑ No
❑ Not applicable

Are the course test items re-examined and evaluated to identify questions answered by all learners or questions not answered by any learners? (Note: Item analysis is a technique to refine test questions. It is not worthwhile to test learners on content they already know or on content that none of them can answer. Test items that are poorly designed can be confusing to learners and therefore unanswerable.)
❑ Yes
❑ No
❑ Not applicable
❑ Other (specify)

Are the test questions (or items) refined after analyzing learners' performance?
❑ Yes
❑ No
❑ Not applicable
❑ Other (specify)

Who grades students' assignments? Check all that apply:

Assignment Types	Graded By				
	Instructor	Tutor	Computer	Other	Not Applicable
Quiz					
Test					
Project					
Discussion forum postings					
Journal reports					
Paper					
Other					

Does the course accept late assignments?
❑ Yes
❑ No
❑ Not applicable
If *yes*, is there any penalty in the form of reduced points for late assignments?
   ❑ Yes
   ❑ No
   ❑ Not applicable

Are students required to submit any one of the following for late assignments?
❑ Reason for late submission (system difficulties, resources not available, etc.)
❑ Doctors statement (if health related)
❑ None
❑ Not applicable

Does the instructor/tutor help students work out a plan to complete their late assignments?
❑ Yes
❑ No
❑ Not applicable
❑ Other (specify)

Are due dates adjusted for students in different time zones?
❑ Yes
❑ No
❑ Not applicable
❑ Other (specify)

Does the course provide an online testing facility?
❑ Yes
❑ No
❑ Not applicable
If *yes*, does the online testing facility include multimedia attributes (e.g., test items are capable of including audio, video, image, etc)?
    ❑ Yes
    ❑ No
    ❑ Not applicable
    ❑ Other (specify)

Check all that apply for the course related exams and tests:

Exam Type	Exam and Test are Given					
	Weekly	*Monthly*	*Mid-Term*	*Term Final*	*Based Learners' Readiness*	*Other*
Take home						
Proctored exam						
Proctored online exam						
Online exam						

Online quizzes (Unannounced)						
Other						

If exams are proctored, how are proctors selected?

If exams are proctored, how are students identification established?

Evaluation types used in the course
- ❑ Self evaluation
- ❑ Peer evaluation
- ❑ Group evaluation
- ❑ Instructor
- ❑ Other
- ❑ Not applicable

Does the institution have policies and guidelines regarding the assessment of students that the course instructor must follow?
- ❑ Yes
- ❑ No
- ❑ Not applicable
- ❑ Other (specify)

Does the course set clear assessment standards?
- ❑ Yes
- ❑ No
- ❑ Not applicable

Does the course use a <u>pretest</u> to assess learners' pre-requisite skills on learning tasks in its various lessons?
- ❑ Yes
- ❑ No
- ❑ Not applicable
- ❑ Other (specify)

Does the course provide <u>practice items</u> for learners on its various lessons?
- ❑ Yes
- ❑ No
- ❑ Not applicable
- ❑ Other (specify)

Does the course provide frequent confirmational and corrective feedback?

❑ Yes
❑ No
❑ Not applicable

Does the course provide remedial activities?
❑ Yes
❑ No
❑ Not applicable
Does the course have a mechanism in which a learner can be truly measured and not cheat?
❑ Yes
❑ No
❑ Not applicable

Does the course provide an environment that rewards individuals or individual work?
❑ Yes
❑ No
❑ Not applicable

Does the course include authentic assessment strategies to evaluate real-world skills?
❑ Yes
❑ No
❑ Not applicable

Are assignments relevant to course objectives/goals?
❑ Yes
❑ No
❑ Not applicable

Are exercises relevant to course objectives/goals?
❑ Yes
❑ No
❑ Not applicable

Does the course provide clear instructions for preparing and submitting assignments?
❑ Yes
❑ No
❑ Not applicable

Does the course penalize participants who do not turn in their assignments on time?
❑ Yes

❏ No
❏ Not applicable

Does the course provide the option for learners to receive graded papers or
assignments electronically?
❏ Yes
❏ No
❏ Not applicable
If *no*, check all that apply:
  ❏ The instructor sends graded assignments to learners via regular mail
  ❏ The instructor sends graded assignments to learners if learners have
      already sent postage-paid envelopes to the instructor
  ❏ The instructor faxes graded assignments to learners
  ❏ The instructor faxes graded assignments to learners if learners pay the cost
  ❏ Learners can pick up graded assignments from the instructor's location
  ❏ Other (specify)

Does the course have a system for keeping records of student progress online?
❏ Yes
❏ No
❏ Not applicable

Does the course have a system for providing student grades online?
❏ Yes
❏ No
❏ Not applicable

Does the course clearly indicate assignment due dates?
❏ Yes
❏ No
❏ Not applicable
If *yes*, are they suited for geographically diverse time-zones?
  ❏ Yes
  ❏ No
  ❏ Not applicable

Can students appeal any marks or points given for quizzes, essays, exams or
assignments that affect their final grade?
❏ Yes
❏ No
❏ Not applicable

ACTIVITIES

1. Suppose you are working for an institution that is planning an e-learning initiative. You have been asked by your institution to develop a position paper with an overview of the comprehensive e-learning process. This paper should help your institution to see the e-learning process from a birds-eye view and provide the realities of an e-learning environment. Let's call the position paper an *e-learning plan*. In developing the e-learning plan, you should consider including as many critical issues as possible encompassing the eight dimensions of the E-Learning Framework discussed in the book. In the book, issues within each dimension of the E-Learning Framework are presented as *questions* that course designers can ask themselves when planning, designing, developing, implementing and evaluating e-learning and blended-learning materials.

Based on your understanding of the e-learning process and items included in this chapter, develop an **e-learning plan** for your institution. The following is a sample outline for an e-learning plan:

Sample Outline for an E-learning Plan

I. E-learning Environment
    In this section, you will rationalize that e-learning is a viable method of providing education and training to learners dispersed all over the world. Therefore, for your target audience, you should:
    - <u>describe</u> e-learning in your own words
    - <u>identify</u> similarities and differences between e-learning and the traditional classroom, and
    - <u>list</u> the advantages of e-learning over the traditional classroom instruction.

II. Institutional Issues
    In this section, you begin with rationalizing the need for an e-learning initiative at your institution and its potential benefits. Then, discuss the following institutional issues whenever applicable (e.g., if your design plan is for a corporate setting, then "financial aid" may not be an issue, whereas for an academic setting it is an important support service issue).
    - ❏ Administrative Affairs
        - ❏ Budgeting and return on investment
        - ❏ Information technology services
        - ❏ Instructional development and media services
        - ❏ Marketing, admissions, graduation, certification and alumni affairs
        - ❏ Organization and change (diffusion, adoption and implementation of innovation)
    - ❏ Academic Affairs
        - ❏ Faculty and staff support
        - ❏ Instructional affairs
        - ❏ Workload, compensation and intellectual property rights
    - ❏ Student Services
        - ❏ Pre-enrollment services
        - ❏ Course and program information
        - ❏ Orientation
        - ❏ Advising
        - ❏ Counseling
        - ❏ Financial Aid

❑ Registration and payment
❑ Bookstore
❑ Library support
❑ Social support network
❑ Tutorial services
❑ Internship and employment services

III.   Technological Issues
Technology issues should include:
- Infrastructure planning
- Assessment of institution's existing technologies and technology plan
- Standards, policies, and guidelines related to hardware, software and other relevant technologies required for e-learning

- Software Requirements

The tables below are provided to help you in completing your E-learning Plan. You may want to use these tables, or altered versions of them, as you work on your project and even as part of your final report.

	Software Name	Required (Req) Or Recommended (Rec)?						*Cost*
		Learner	Instructor	Tech Support	Institution	Other	*(List specific tasks performed by software)*	
Word processor								
Email package								
Presentation program								
Spreadsheets								
Database								
Authoring tools or LMS*								
Discussion software								
Operating system								
Plug-ins								
Browsers								
ASP								

AV Streaming								
Other								
Comments								

* Learning Management System. Indicate whether LMS is SCORM or IEEE compliance.

- Hardware Requirements

The tables below are provided to help you in completing your E-learning Plan. You may want to use these tables, or altered versions of them, as you work on your project and even as part of your final report.

CPU							
RAM							
ROM							
Hard disk		gigabyte					
Disk drive							
CD-ROM			24x, 32x				
SDRAM	32/64/128 /256MB						
Sound card							
Speaker							
Microphone							
Video card							
DVD							
Ethernet							
Dial-in modem			28.8, 33.6. 56 Kbps				
DSL							
Cable modem							
Wireless Internet connection							
Monitor				12" 14" 16" Other	640X480 800X600 1024X768 256, thousands, millions		
Ink-jet							
Laser							
Digital camera							
Video camera							
Other							
Comments							

Note: Type L=Learner, I=Instructor, T=Tutor, S=Technical Support and IN=Institution wherever applies in the above Table.

IV.   Pedagogical and Evaluation Issues
- Discuss the instructional approach (unstructured vs. structured learning activities) for designing the course content. Here, you can describe how the overall design of learning activities for various parts of the course content can be developed: highly structured, mostly structured, loosely structured or unstructured.

- Provide a brief description of at least five of the following instructional methods emphasizing how they are used successfully in courses (provide course URLs).
  Presentation
  Demonstration
  Drill and Practice
  Tutorials
  Games
  Story Telling
  Simulations
  Role-playing
  Discussion
  Interaction
  Modeling
  Facilitation
  Collaboration
  Debate
  Field Trips
  Apprenticeship
  Case Studies
  Generative Development
  Motivation

- Discuss how learner assessment will be designed?
- Discuss how instructor evaluation will be conducted?
- Discuss how the design of the learning environment will be assessed?

V.   Interface Design and Ethical Issues
- Discuss interface design issues including site design, navigation and usability testing for e-learning.
- Discuss ethical considerations that should be taken into account in designing e-learning; including, social and cultural diversity, bias, geographical diversity, learner diversity, information accessibility, etiquette and legal issues (e.g., policies and guidelines, privacy, plagiarism and copyright).

VI.   Resource Support and Management issues
- Discuss online support services including instructional, counseling and career guidance.
- Discuss both online and offline resources available for e-learning.
- Discuss the maintenance of e-learning sites and the distribution of information.

VII. E-Learning Case Studies
- Using the Internet's search engines, identify and write about two or three existing e-learning programs that encompasses many of the issues covered in the above outlines.

2. Many organizations including corporations, government agencies, nonprofits, and educational institutions are currently using e-learning and blended-learning materials for their various educational and training programs. Using the checklist items in this chapter, conduct a **program evaluation** of an online program.

REFERENCES

Boshier, R., Mohapi, M., Moulton, G., Qayyum, A., Sadownik, L. & Wilson, M. (1997). Best and worst dressed web courses: Strutting into the 21st Century in comfort and style, *Distance Education*, 18(2), 327-348.

About the Author

Badrul H. Khan, Ph.D., is an international speaker, author, educator and consultant in the field of e-learning and educational technology. Dr. Khan authored the following books: *Web Based Instruction* (1997), *Web Based Training* (2001), *E-Learning Strategies* (2004), *E-Learning QUICK Checklist* (2005), *Managing E-Learning* (2005), *Flexible Learning* (2005). *Implementing E-Learning* (in press), *E-Learning: Design, Delivery and Evaluation* (in press*), E-Learning and Blended Learning Strategies* (in press). A sought-after  keynote speaker on e-learning, Khan is past president of the International Division of the Association for Educational and Communication Technology (AECT). He served as a consultant/advisor to distance education-related projects at the World Bank, Ministry of Education in several countries, and academic institutions and corporations in the USA and abroad. Dr. Khan is Director of the Educational Technology Leadership graduate cohort program at the George Washington University. He is founder of ***BooksToRead.com***, a recommended readings site on the Internet.